Charismatic Connection

Whispers of A Love That Transcends Time

Charismatic Connection

Whispers of A Love That Transcends Time

Serena Jade

The House of Raising The Sparks, New York

ISBN- 9798218686192

Library of Congress number: TX 7-988-347

Cover photographs © by Serena Jade
Some names have been changed for the protection of the person's identity.
Chris Antley's own words are marked by a footnote.

To you, my dear friends

In Celebration of Charismatic Connection...

"You will enjoy reading this book to the end and learn something about yourself as well. Hat's off to Serena Jade! Pick up a copy today. I was given this book by Smith Publicity Inc."- Maryanne Koopmann (Book Reviewer) - Reviews for Amazon.com, GoodReads.com and BarnesandNoble.com.

"Charismatic Connection is a beautifully written [story] in which the main characters are soul mates who meet again and recognize each other at a deep spiritual level long before their lives become intertwined through thoroughbred racing. They are both protagonists with deep sorrow in their immediate lives, seeking solace but constantly torn from the immediate connection and pull they felt towards each other from time immemorial. The book is truly for romantics and horse lovers, as the plot is revealed through the running of many well-known horse races and events that keep bringing the two main characters into contact with each other, in ever-deepening ways. The book is one that will keep you reading to the end,with amazing spiritual overtones in a way that will draw you in."- Bonnie Neely, Real Travel Adventures Magazine Editor

"The device of telling the twin stories of Serena Jade and Chris Antley using alternating narrators works, especially in that it creates a sense of immediacy and intimacy. Readers feel as if they have been given a unique and privileged window into the hearts and minds of two people. Experiencing the stories in this way means that by the end of the book, readers feel they truly understand the suffering both Serena and Chris have withstood, as well as your struggles to transcend the limitations and weaknesses of their less formed selves."-Francesca, CreateSpace Editor

Table of Contents

This is a true story. From the moment Chris and I first met, our souls recognized each other. Many people think a soul mate is an ordinary social interaction, and most don't see the world in a way that ties their passion to their soul mate's passion. My story is about my passion to horses and racing, not yours as the reader. I encourage the reader to explore their soul's passion.

The essence of this book is that Chris and I awoke from a deep sleep, recognizing each other from an eternal connection. This recognition wasn't familiar to our conscious minds (ego), nor did it feel like we had known each other all our lives—a common misconception by those who confuse the personality (ego) with soul recognition. In an ordinary attraction, it feels like home and resonates with the personality (ego). However, the bond Chris and I shared was rooted in our deepest, most profound essence—our souls. The soul is timeless, formless, infinite, and transcends time itself.

Chris passed away on December 2, 2000. On March 11, 2025, I dreamed of him again. It had been so long since the last time, and I woke up feeling grateful for the visit from his soul—gentle whispers of a love that transcends time. - Serena Jade, May 2025

Preface

Many moons ago in a legendary land, the delicious north and west winds created mountains and waterfalls, while a seductive breeze from the east swirled the sands of eternity into being. The sultry southern air blew with such intensity that the ancient desert witnessed the Divine forming a profound masterpiece, the Fertile Crescent of the Middle East; giving birth to human civilization, as well as to the horse.

The Arabian horse is a gift from the heavenly sphere for Homo sapiens. God knew that humans would only survive in the vastness of this land if they possessed a means of transportation, so in the infinite sands of the Fertile Crescent, the ruling spirit blew life into the nostrils of the Arabian.

Thousands of years later, the Arabian's descendants share a genetic code with the most exquisite, intelligent, swift creature on this planet: the thoroughbred racehorse.

In the seventeenth century, three Arabian stallions, the Darley Arabian, the Godolphin Arabian, and the Beyerly Turk, were shipped to England from the Middle East, and were then mated with the best English mares. This breeding produced the purest and the best horse in the world, known today as the thoroughbred.

Thoroughbreds are extremely high strung, graceful, and sleek, with lively, sparkling eyes. Their heads and arched necks are full of power and determination. Their nostrils flare with the air, while their rich manes flow with the wind. Their strong muscles are defined, and their legs are deceptively vulnerable and delicate. They are truly among the most magnificent, elegant animals on this earth. Don't be fooled by their beauty: they can also be dangerous. Thoroughbreds will bite, lunge, kick, buck, or rear up without notice.

I fell in love with the thoroughbred and racing at a very young age. My father Louis had a passion for the Sport of Kings, and he used to take me to the races, for as long as I can remember. I was dazzled by the speed and the radiance of these awesome beings. To see a thoroughbred racehorse up close is to see a supreme example of a living piece of art.

The sport of horse racing was well liked in the 1930s, 1940s, and 1950s. My father would tell me the whole grandstand and clubhouse of the racetrack used to be filled with thousands of people at that time. Horse racing is an international sport, although in the United States, it has declined in the interest of the general public over the years.

There is one horse race that is still very popular in America, and that is the Kentucky Derby. If a layperson has never watched a horse race in their life, they will probably at some point watch the Kentucky Derby. If you are lucky enough to go to the Kentucky Derby, it will be an experience you will never forget.

I followed my passion for horses and racing, and down the road a soul mate crossed paths with mine. I was spellbound by him, and he was mesmerized by me. Chris Antley was a well-known American jockey, and I was a stable hand, and we shared the same exalted inner essence. Our connection exuded an intensity that transcended the time and space between us. There was one problem that kept us apart. We knew we were not worthy of such a deep and profound love.

Charismatic Connection interweaves the parallel stories of Chris Antley and myself. As we enter the world of horse racing, we spiritually wake up. Our thirst is racehorses, and we live through our trauma and tragedy.

My goal is for you to understand your spiritual essence. I would like you to realize that until your personality has transcended its pain and suffering, your immortal soul cannot express its wisdom. If you have a desire to mate at a very high spiritual level, your personality must be up to par with your everlasting being.

I hope to give you the inspiration to look within and discover yourself. I would also like to encourage you to reach for a relationship that is beyond a need for security, for the truth is we must know our own value, and cannot elevate our self-worth by using another person. You will then be ready for “Charismatic Connections” with yourself, others, and the world! So come along with me, and experience the journey that Chris and I have taken. Together let us arise from unawareness to discover a genuine soul mate connection…

Chapter 1

Serena

On a spring night during my thirty-second year on this earth, I have a very vivid dream. My subconscious mind is showing me I am in the countryside of England. My mother has just died, and I am grieving uncontrollably. I miss her so much—I am about sixteen years old, and I will never see my mother again. I feel the one thing that is going to help me through this time in my life is my love for horses. My brother Michael and I help my father with the chores around the house, but in our spare time we love to gallop the brilliant colts in our barn.

I am a beautiful, dark-haired, slim girl and my brother Michael is a tall, brown-eyed, slender man. I love my brother's friend, Lyle. He is a handsome man with beautiful eyes and a sculpted body. Lyle, Michael, and I are riding in foxhunt meets. All three of us love to ride for hours on end. Our special bond is our love for horses, and we gallop our horses like we are in heaven. I'm riding sidesaddle on my prized colt, and feel magnificent, as if I'm riding Pegasus in a mythical land. It's wonderful to have the two people I adore riding with me.

On one particular summer day, Lyle and I go out for a gallop on our own. Lyle is riding his strong, black thoroughbred stallion with the markings of a star on his forehead. This horse knows he is a star; he is a descendant from the Byerly Turk stallion. I am riding an elegant, graceful, dark-brown English filly with very few markings on her.

Lyle and I are immersed in the rolling hills of the countryside. The grass is a hunter green, and the trees have filled out with their lush leaves. We are on top of the mound of earth. It is sunny, and I cherish the warmth against my skin. We are fully in this moment, enjoying each other's company. He says, "Let's stop and let our horses rest."

Then he says, "Let's take a stroll," and we walk hand in hand; we stop and look deeply into each other's eyes. He says, "I can see the heavenly light in your eyes—I love you."

My heart is fluttering with excitement. I say, "I love you too, with all my heart and soul." We are kissing with such intense bliss, and holding each other so tightly, we don't want to let go.

Our horses love the break, and are grazing on the grass. We decide to lie down so we put a blanket underneath us. We lovingly gaze into each other's eyes. He kisses me again on the lips, and I love it. He has something to tell me, and I don't like the sound of his voice. He says he is going away, and is getting married.

My heart plummets into the pit of my stomach. I am utterly devastated. He says, "I know we are deeply connected, and we will meet again. I know that for sure, but I need to marry this woman. The arrangement is an obligation to my family. I hate to tell you this, but I am moving to Scotland."

"Scotland…why Scotland?" I yell in disbelief.

He replies, "Scotland is where her family lives. We have a blessed bond, and I will always have you in my heart. We are like Scotch tape; I will always be stuck on you. When I am with her, it's you I will be thinking about; my heart will always be with you. When I'm riding my gorgeous stallion, I will always know that you will be close to your horse too. Our love for horses will be our connecting link."

I blurt out, "I know you have an obligation to your family, but what about us? I don't know what I am going to do without you. I know we have a divinely-inspired relationship. I can see the celestial glimmer in your eyes too. I know we share a bond in horses. When I am riding, I know you will be riding somewhere too."

Lyle promises that we are going to meet again, and that we will remember each other.

I wake up; it is three in the morning.

Chapter 2

Serena

I get up, and write down my dream. The luminosity of the images in my mind is so strikingly real. Did this scenario happen before? Or is it going to take place in the future? Could it have existed in the past? Do you believe in having a past life memory? I feel it could have occurred in another lifetime.

I am dreaming about a man I am in love with, who tells me he can see heaven in my eyes. I don't have a conscious clue. Is he a love I have for someone real, but for now, existing only in my unconscious mind, waiting for when the time is right?

My deep admiration for horses and racing has to originate from somewhere. Does my enthusiasm come from being exposed to the sport at a young age? I had such a great relationship with my father, who taught me to love horses when I was a child. Or perhaps my warmth for horses is an ancient memory from the sensuous lure of the Middle East?

I grew up on the South Shore of Long Island, New York. I don't live in Kentucky, where horse racing is in one's back yard. One thing I know for sure: horse racing saved me from my dysfunctional childhood. My desire to be with the thoroughbred consumed my whole life. At age ten, I begin dreaming of becoming a jockey and fantasizing about it.

≈

Chapter 3

Serena

The sun is brilliant on a cool spring day in New York City in the year 1966. Many people view this city as the king of the world, and like every royal ruler, this king has his queen. Queens is one of the five boroughs of the metropolitan area. Ozone Park is in the heart of Queens and is home to a thoroughbred racetrack, and the residence of my parents.

On this first day in April, better known as April Fools' Day, a practical joke doesn't happen; rather, an old soul is about to enter the world. My forty-six-year-old mother Elizabeth gives birth to me, to the great pleasure of my father, forty-seven-year-old Louis.

My father is of medium to small stature, at five feet, seven inches tall and 130 pounds, with dark brown hair and dark brown eyes. A quiet, aloof man, he was born in Brooklyn, New York in January in the year 1919.

My grandfather, Frank, was born in Buenos Aires. His father, Antonio, left Italy in the late 1800s and boarded a ship sailing to Argentina. Antonio attended an art school in Buenos Aires, and became a sculptor. As time marched on, Antonio fell in love with Rosa, an Argentinean woman. Rosa gave birth to my grandfather, Frank, but soon passed away, leaving my great-grandfather alone with a four-year-old son.

Antonio decided to leave Buenos Aires and sail back to Italy, settling in Migliacino, some fifty miles northeast of Bologna. As time passed my great-grandfather married again, and had four more children. Years later, Frank and his half brothers emigrated to the United States of America.

Mary, my grandmother, came from Arienza in the Campania region of southern Italy and met Frank in Brooklyn, New York. They married on January 12, 1913, and had six children, including my father Louis. My grandmother had a submissive personality that attracted my grandfather into her life. My grandfather was overpowering, and my docile father took after his mother. My father had to be passive to live with my mother.

My father had to leave school at fifteen, to help support his family financially. When my father was twenty-two years old, he volunteered to serve in the army, as World War II had just begun. He was stationed in England and France during the war. In England, his infantry rode horses up mountains and camped in the cold weather.

My father hated having to face the freezing temperature, but he was a brave solider on the beaches of Normandy. Fighting in this horrific battle, he received a Purple Heart for being shot in his gluteus maximus. In the end, he survived the war, witnessing much cruelty along the way, and when he returned home he was a changed man.

My father didn't believe in himself, and had no education to speak of, so when he came home, he didn't know how to make a good living. He therefore became a laborer and worked very hard. I come from a working class family and my father showed me how to have a great work ethic. I admire his integrity and share his solid values.

Before he met my mother, my father dated a woman he caught cheating on him. Walking in on her and her lover, he was devastated. Soon after that incident he met my mother; they started to date, and soon after they married. My father was thirty-five and my mother thirty-four when they tied the knot on a hot June day in the year 1954. They had two children within the first three years of their marriage, my sisters, Mary Lou and Francine. I came along nine years later.

My father enjoyed having a third child at an older age, and we bonded from the start. My father's passion both before the war and after was horse racing—it was his favorite pastime. When my father was growing up in the 1930s, horse racing was the number-one spectator sport.

He remembers watching War Admiral win the 1937 Triple Crown. The Triple Crown consists of three prestigious races in five weeks: the spectacular Kentucky Derby, the Preakness Stakes, and the Belmont Stakes. He also remembers watching the match race between War Admiral and Seabiscuit, and talks about the race like it was yesterday.

He loved the legendary Hall of Fame jockey Eddie Arcaro, the two-time winner of horse racing's Triple Crown aboard Whirlaway in 1941, and Citation in 1948. His favorite jockey of all time is Hall-of-Famer Teddy Atkinson. Teddy Atkinson was the first jockey ever to win one million dollars in purse money in a season. He was the leading rider in the United States in 1944 and 1946.

My father considers Kelso the greatest horse he has ever seen run. Kelso did not compete in the Kentucky Derby in 1960, but won the title of Horse of the Year from 1960–1964, the only horse ever to win the title five times in a row. Kelso is fourth behind Citation, Secretariat, and Man o'War in the list of the greatest racehorses of all time.

Horse racing is in my father's blood, and he passed that passion for horses and racing on to me. I adore my father, and we have a special bond: that shared link is horse racing.

Chapter 4

Serena

Elizabeth, my mother, is in her room, standing in front of the magic mirror. She is looking at herself, and she says, "I am beautiful, with my lustrous hair, light brown eyes, and attractive figure." This reflection reminds her to always look her best, and to never let her hair turn gray.

The looking glass says to Elizabeth, "You have a daughter, who looks a lot like you."

"I know she looks like me, but mirror, mirror on the wall, who is the superior one of all?"

"Of course you are, Elizabeth."

I will never have her approval to be my own person. If I try to outdo her in looks or life, she will be envious of me. This feels like death: my mother doesn't want to see her own offspring sparkle. So I hide the real me.

My mother was born on a hot August day in Brooklyn, New York, in 1920. Her parents were from the Campania region of southern Italy, and emigrated to the United States when they were in their twenties.

My grandfather is on the short side, with dark brown hair. He was a very mean, domineering, narcissistic, strict man. My grandmother is short, with brown hair turning gray. She is very passive and withdrawn. My mother takes after her father: I would absolutely define my mother as a mean, domineering, narcissistic, strict person—just like him.

My mother is holding me in her arms and looking at me, projecting what she needs onto me. Most mothers look into the eyes of their child, and see a beautiful, special little person. Most mothers are not like my mother.

Elizabeth has a full-blown narcissistic personality. She has a grandiose sense of self-importance; she believes she is special, requires excessive admiration, and has a sense of entitlement. She takes advantage of her kids (especially me), displays arrogance, and worst of all, demonstrates a lack of empathy (especially towards me).[i]

I don't have a mother who sees me as her precious little jewel. Rather, I have a mother who projects onto me her expectations of what I can do for her. This sets me up for a life of psychological distress, emotional pain, and suffering. I want and need my mother's respect and understanding, and I am constantly trying to obtain these essential needs from her, but she is incapable of giving them to me. She gave me one important value in life—to please her.

I am under my mother's power since day one. Elizabeth can and will abuse me as she sees fit. Living with a narcissistic mother is like hell on Earth. All the members of my family revolve around Elizabeth, contributing to her sense of self-importance. My father is very passive, and accepts his unwritten role to take care of my mother. My two sisters, Mary Lou and Fran, revolve around my mother as well. My sisters are afraid of my mother, and will not talk back to her. My sisters feel they are more significant than me, and can talk to me in a demeaning way.

My mother is the most important person in the family. My father is second in line. My sisters are third, and I am valued the least. I am the "bad daughter," while my sisters are "good." I have all the defects, while my sisters have the virtues. Somehow I have become the scapegoat for my family, and am considered an outcast. My mother labels me as different; she cannot stand that I represent feeling when she herself cannot feel. Yet I want to be accepted by my mother and sisters, so I take abuse from them while they continue to take advantage of me.

I take the blame for the issues my mother disowns, and that causes me to repress my vulnerable nature. I am both mentally and emotionally impoverished, which leads me to have a very low sense of self-worth. At two years old I was already learning to be a people pleaser, so when my mother says "No," it's "No."

This sets the course of my life; other people will easily manipulate me, and the first person who does so is my mother. I learn to distrust that my needs will ever be met. I can't rely on my family for their support.

I can't count on my mother for her loving touch or embrace, so I create what is called a fantasy bond. I imagine I have a warm loving mother who embraces and loves me. This is just make-believe, as I learn to parent and protect myself. I grow up quite independent, but it is a defense mechanism, knowing I can't depend on "Mommy Dearest."

Chapter 5

Serena

I'm outside of my parents' house on a breezy spring day. I am three years old, and my friend and I are playing tag. We are laughing, and enjoying each other's companionship. My friend runs through the front door of my house, and I follow; then with a swift movement, he runs back outside, and I am right behind him.

All of a sudden, I am screaming at the top of my lungs. My little pinky finger is caught in the door as it is closing. I am shouting, "It hurts so much—make it stop!" But my friend, who is the same age as me, keeps trying to shut the door. My mother hears my cry of pain, and comes rushing to see what's happening.

She sees my friend still closing the door, and yells at him to stop. My friend listens, and my mother pulls me away, but she is frantic and doesn't know what to do. Blood is everywhere, but I'm feeling so much pain I don't even notice. My mother puts a towel over my hand and rushes me to the doctor across the street. Tears are rolling down my face as we reach the doctor's.

My mother doesn't have the empathy to sense how I'm feeling, so she sits me on the chair next to her. She is holding my bloody hand with the towel. We see the doctor and he takes a look at my hand. The tip of my pinky finger is completely chopped off and is dangling like a piece of thread. The doctor tells my mother, "You need to go to the hospital, and have them sew it back on."

My mother doesn't drive, so she calls my father and tells him, "You need to leave work early and take us to the hospital."

My father says, "I'll come as quickly as I can." My father is in Manhattan at this point and rushes home to Queens. An hour has passed, and my mother and I are still in Queens waiting for my father.

I am saying to myself, "I can't handle the pain; I want the agony to go away." I am yelling, "Where is Daddy?" Finally he comes, and we get in his car, I am crying, sitting all alone in the back seat. We get to the cold and sterile hospital. The nurse directs us to a room. My mother doesn't go in the room with my father and me. She waits outside in the waiting area. I'm so scared. I can hear the doctor talking to my father, and the next thing I know, my father leaves me all alone. I am crying hysterically, "Daddy, don't leave me alone. Daddy! Daddy, don't leave."

The doctor gives me a shot, and I turn around and he is putting my hand in a sterile cup. He begins to sew my finger back together. I don't know how long it takes. It feels like an eternity, but it's all over now. My father comes back into the room, but now I am traumatized. The doctor says, "Her finger should heal well."

My father picks me up, and is carrying me to the car. My mother gets into the front seat. My father puts me in the backseat, so I'm sitting by myself again. I feel like a castaway, very alone and scared on a deserted island. I experience a lot of trauma, not only physical pain, but psychological abandonment by my mother and father. I don't feel I deserve my mother's safe support.

I am dismissed, so I feel like I am not worthy of her touch. My father leaving me alone doesn't make me feel secure either. Emotionally, I am alone in life, as I'm hurt, angry, and frightened. My emotional needs are not getting met, and I don't feel protected from danger. My memory of this day will fade, but I will feel the deep pain and emptiness within me for a very long time.

Chapter 6

Chris

The waves are thundering to the shore, and the beaches in Fort Lauderdale, Florida have awakened. The sun in all its glory is beaming, and the palm trees are swaying. It's 1:12 p.m. eastern time, and a six-pound, twelve-ounce, nineteen-and-a-half-inch baby is born. Les and Michelle are so happy. Their little boy is here. Today is January 6, 1966, the day their son will receive a gift.

The sixth of January is the Feast of the Epiphany, a day which celebrates the last day of Christmas. This holiday does not get a lot of attention in the United States, but halfway around the world, it's 7:12 p.m. in Italy. People are celebrating, gathering at the Piazza Navona in Rome. The square is filled with balloons and festive lights, and vendors are selling food and candy. Everyone is having a blast as they laugh, eat, and drink. On this date, the wise men traveled to Bethlehem to bring divine presents of myrrh (wisdom for the world), frankincense (intuitive understanding), and gold (a comprehension of our spiritual essence) to the mortal baby Jesus.

A legend was born in this European country sometime in a distant past. A good witch would skip around on rooftops, slide down chimneys, and leave gifts for children on the eve of the holiday. Kids are always excited to find presents waiting for them when they wake on January the sixth.

Back in the United States, an old soul has arrived on earth: his name is Christopher Wiley Antley. Chris is a beautiful baby, with deep blue-green eyes that sparkle like gems. He is a gift to this world, and has a present to share. Chris is the oldest of three children born to Les and Michelle Antley. His mother Michelle is a blond, petite woman who is overpowering, and takes every opportunity to be critical. His father, a rather good-looking man, is somewhat withdrawn and distant.

I'm Chris and I'm growing up in Fort Lauderdale, Florida. I love to feel the warmth of the sun. My parents take me to the beach, and I'm having fun jumping the waves. Awesome! I have a natural affinity with water—being around its energy just makes me happy.

When I'm at home, I don't have a sense of ease. I can feel that my family life is chaotic. Soon after my brother is born, he begins to develop the traits of my mother, while I have the characteristics of my father. At two, I start to develop my people-pleasing ways.

I can feel the crispness in the air; autumn is here. You can see it in my eyes. I'm thrilled about the road trip we're going on tomorrow. We are off to a family gathering, and we're going to be celebrating Thanksgiving. My father is driving north on Highway 95, heading towards Sumter, South Carolina. My relatives are going deer hunting, and I want to go with them but I am too young. I'm disappointed, but I can't comprehend that the gun is bigger than I am! I'm ashamed I am not taller and stronger, and wonder if I'll grow up to be an average height. I guess only time will tell.

As time goes on, my mother and father aren't getting along, and talk about making a move. I watch the seasons pass, and before I know it, I've reached the age of six. My family and I move to a very small, quaint town in South Carolina, where we settle into a small house that needs fixing. The rural area of Elloree only has a population of about 700. Cotton fields stretch as far as the eye can see, and Spanish moss spreads from tree to tree. It's a location to kick back and relax, a place to raise a family in peace, but only if your own mindset is serene.

Fast-forward a year, and a light snow is falling as Christmas arrives in the South. I receive my first bow and arrow set—it's as if I have been given a sign to acquire the skills that will enable me to one day awaken an eternal love.

I'm here in Carolina. Open fields surround me and, in the distance, horses romp freely. I love watching a couple of fillies as they buck and play. When I get up on my first horse, he runs off with me, and I swear never to get back up on a horse in my life.

My family life is becoming more chaotic. My mother finds fault with almost everything about me. I feel I am not worthy of her love. Intense shame penetrates me, creating in me an inferiority complex.

In the middle of the night, I wake up to pounding rain. I hear my parents arguing about having a third child, and a year later my mother is pregnant. My parents have been getting into ugly power struggles, and eventually decide it's best for the family if they call it quits. I am twelve years old when my parents decide to divorce.

I am emotionally distraught seeing my family ripped apart right before my eyes. Tears roll down my face, for I don't want my father to leave. I'm shouting, "Please Dad, don't leave." But he does leave, and now I just don't feel safe or secure. Home life is extremely important to me.

The number six I feel to be very auspicious. The symbol six fuses together the foundation of family, home, love, and harmony. In numerology, if you are connected with the number six, and you don't have a functional family, there is a sense of emptiness. I am a person who needs balance and family around me to give me support, and I don't have that.

In years to come, I will be standing by the rail of the racetrack at Belmont Park conversing with a trainer. I say to Nick, "A lot of us have problems, but there are some children out there who need special guidance." Nick says I was one of those children. Whenever someone comes along and gives me support, it puts me back on the right path.[ii]

Deep down I need to feel that I am worthy, not made to feel unsafe from put-downs. I don't have the tools to develop a strong emotional sense of self. My parents cannot give me the family life and the emotional security that I need; yet they are the only ones who can fulfill those essential needs.[iii]

I look at my family life, and I sure don't remember any scenes like those happy family dinners. I want to say I remember all those good, typical, happy childhood things. But I don't.[iv] I have a lot of feelings within me, but I am not expressing them. My hurt and anger, where are they going? Right down the rabbit hole, nowhere to be found, but they will come back to haunt me sooner or later.

What about the gift I have to share with you? I was born with the ability to be in touch with my sixth sense, to access the gift of knowledge from the spiritual realms. But it is the 1970s, and just the mention of having a sixth sense will send you right to the witch trials, especially in the little town of Elloree, where everyone knows your business. Here, the idea of a sixth sense doesn't enter people's minds.

Nonetheless, I am a five-foot, one-inch, freckled, dimpled, dirty-blond-haired, blue-green-eyed kid from South Carolina, and I have a psychic gift. I will prove to the world that having this gift sets me apart from everyone else.

Chapter 7

Serena

I am learning to keep my anger, hurt, and fear to myself. I know I cannot express what I truly feel, as this defense keeps me from feeling overwhelmed. I am learning to numb myself so I can survive. My blocked emotions are leading me in a downward spiral; I don't feel safe, and I have a shortage of confidence.

My parents lack the parenting skills I need to grow up to be confident and secure. A few months after my traumatic finger accident, my family and I move from Queens to Oceanside, Long Island. I have a couple of friends in Queens, and I like playing with them, but I am now living in a different situation.

The houses on Long Island are more spread out and isolated, as opposed to Queens where people live very closely packed together. There, people hang out on their stoops day and night, but on Long Island no one sits on their steps—it is just very different.

My aunt and uncle and my cousin, who is fifteen years older than me, live just around the corner from my new house. The great part about living in Oceanside is that I'm just ten minutes from the beach! My only companion now is my mother, but she is so self-absorbed that when I want to talk to her, she just says, "Leave me alone." My mother and sisters never have any respect for my voice or me. Soon I become introverted in response to my mother's self-involvement.

My sister loves that she can overpower me by talking for me. I learn very early on that I cannot trust my mother or sisters, and that I can't rely on my father for that much either, as he is controlled by my mother as well. Sometimes my father stands up for me, which my mother despises, accusing me of being spoiled.

Here we have a three year old who has no one to depend on. I grow up projecting a powerful tough girl, but I'm really not strong—it's just a way to avoid appearing vulnerable to my mother or sisters. My mother is creating a co-dependent relationship with me. My whole identity is what I can do for her. In this dysfunctional system, I'm taking care of my mother in exchange for her love. My mother is neglecting to take care of and revere her own daughter!

My mother is in her late forties, but her mental and emotional state is in her adolescent years. Emotionally, she is very unpredictable: one minute she is up, and then the next minute she is down. My relationships with other people are now set in motion based on the unhealthy model established within my own family: I attract people based on what can I do for them, at the expense of taking care of myself.

I never feel comfortable being introverted, and always feel the desire within to become more extroverted. My lack of confidence prevents me from opening up. However, I use my disadvantage to good use, and I am able to tap into my intuitive mind. I don't know it yet, but my sixth sense is what will help me throughout my life.

Chapter 8

Serena

By the time I am sent off to kindergarten, I have spent two years in isolation with my mother. Can you imagine what I was experiencing on my first day of school? I felt like I was being whisked away all alone to a foreign land at the ripe old age of five.

The teardrops are falling from my eyes as I leave home and enter a new world. My sobbing continues throughout the school year. Another student asks me, “What is wrong?” I can’t give her an answer. I feel all alone and abandoned, but I don’t know how to articulate what I am feeling.

School is torture for me. I don’t have the necessary social skills, and this makes it hard to interact with my peers. Although my personality is identified as introverted, deep down I want to be social, but I don’t know how. I definitely don’t have confidence in myself. On almost every report card from kindergarten through the fifth grade my teachers write, “She needs more confidence.” What does my mother do with this information? She says at home I have a big mouth. So I don’t feel safe either at home or in school. I lack security, and I don’t want to exist in the here and now.

I am always attracting teachers who are cold and strict, just like my mother. I want to escape the reality I am living in! On top of all of this, I am getting bullied at home by my mother and two sisters. At school, a bunch of girls bully me as well, calling me names and making fun of me before classes start. Ironically, my older sister Mary Lou comes to school and tells them to leave me alone.

The girls get the message, and I end up becoming very good friends with one of them. I don’t want to experience reality, so I dive into my imagination and get lost in the abyss of my mind. This is not the ideal way to use my mind—my mind is undisciplined and I simply use my ability to escape. In other words, I am fantasizing, and don't pay attention to what is going on in the classroom.

At home, I am the caretaker of my mother. I am also bearing the brunt of my mother's anger, rejection, and betrayal, as this is the norm. I am set apart from my sisters and I internalize the guilt like I am somehow responsible for Mommy's anger. I cry to myself and say, "No one loves me." I am the chosen one, and I learn to please and care for my mother's emotional needs. Then I take the blame for the issues my mother cannot understand, such as her anger.

Chapter 9

Serena

Sundays are the day of the week my family and I go to the races. When I lived in Ozone Park, Queens, I was right down the block from Aqueduct Racetrack. I remember once or twice going to the races, but I was very young, and the thoroughbred had not yet made a big impression on my life.

I am now at Belmont Park, around twenty minutes from my home in Oceanside. It's a warm and sunny day, and I am playing by myself in the grandstand of the racetrack. I have lived on this earth for six revolutions, and I'm picking up discarded losing tickets.

My father brings me to the rail of the racetrack, and together we are watching a horse race. The horses' hooves are roaring around the turn and heading for home, as the jockeys' whips make a powerful cracking sound. My father is yelling, "Come on Cruguet! Come on Jean!" Jean Cruguet is the jockey on the winning horse. I think my father knows the jockey, not understanding at the time that he is rooting for the horse he bet on to win—and that he won.

Incidentally, Jean Cruguet will ride Seattle Slew a couple of years hence in my favorite Derby prep race, the Flamingo Stakes, and win by five lengths. They will go on to win the Triple Crown, as Seattle Slew is the only undefeated thoroughbred in horse racing history to win racing's most prestigious races.

It is thrilling to me that a woman jockey is in this race. Her name is Robyn Smith, who in a few years will be the wife of the famed dancer Fred Astaire. On this day, I know in my heart that I want to be a jockey, and in this realization, my love of horse racing is born. Within the next year, I will watch the greatest racehorse in the history of the sport win the Triple Crown of racing: the great and awesome Secretariat.

I'm seven years old and I don't fully wrap my head around this historic moment in racing history. It's 1973, and I am watching the Kentucky Derby with my father. Secretariat is galloping towards the finish line, and wins this famed horse race. The superhorse Secretariat sets a track record for the mile and a quarter at 1:59:40—that's one minute, fifty-nine and two-fifths seconds, a record that still holds today. Secretariat goes on to win the Preakness Stakes, the second jewel of the Triple Crown, and breaks another record. The time for that race is disputed as the clock stopped, so no one knows for sure how fast the race was run. Nonetheless, Secretariat wins the Preakness Stakes.

Three weeks go by, and Secretariat does it again, winning the Belmont Stakes, the third leg of the Triple Crown, by thirty-one lengths. He set a track record that still stands today for the mile and a half race: 2.24.00. My father and I watch all these races, and are enjoying the excitement.

Months go by until September is upon us, and I realize what a fabulous horse Secretariat is. I am at Belmont Park with my family, and I see Secretariat run in person. I am yelling, "Come on, Secretariat! Come on!" I will never forget watching this famed racehorse so easily win the Man o'War Stakes.

Two years fly by, and it's a hot summer day in July of 1975, when my family and I are visiting my aunt Lena and uncle Rocco. They live around the corner from my family home in Oceanside. The sky is blue as we are celebrating my aunt and uncle's wedding anniversary and enjoying a barbeque in their backyard. This day was talked about for months in the horse-racing world. It is the match race of the decade and perhaps of the twentieth century. My uncle Rocco hooks up a television outside so we can all watch the race.

Ruffian, the undefeated filly, and the Kentucky Derby winner, Foolish Pleasure, are about to enter the magical race at Belmont Park. They break out of the gate; the first quarter is run at a fast pace, and Ruffian is ahead by a nose. She is looking like she is going to beat Foolish Pleasure, when her right foreleg snaps.

We are all horrified when Ruffian goes down—my father can't believe it. That was the last match race I remember ever seeing in the sport. Ruffian was immediately taken to the hospital and operated upon, but she did not recover, and had to be euthanized the next day. Ruffian is buried in the infield at Belmont Park.

Nine months from now I will be ten years old, and totally absorbed in the world of horse racing. I am daydreaming about becoming a jockey, but I have yet to get on a horse!

Chapter 10

Serena

I'm not happy at home or at school, and never pick up a book and read. I don't have the knowledge. I am just living out my mother's message to me that I am not good enough, so why should I even bother? I sabotage my education and seek admiration from strangers, trying desperately to make up for what my mother cannot give me.

One day in my twelfth year, I am especially frustrated, as my mother will not let me hang out with my friends. My father brought home a book weeks ago, so I take a look at the back cover and am intrigued. Crying and alone, I hide in my closet, and I start to read an entire book by choice for the first time. It was titled: *Sometimes, I Don't Love My Mother.*

How ironic. The story is about a mother and daughter. The mother is dependent on her daughter after her husband dies, while the daughter feels guilty and resentful that her mother is not allowing her to live her own life. I know I have to read this book, and finish it in one day! It's as if my father, by giving me this book, wished to say, "I know what you are going through."

You see, I'm not focused in school, but I will do everything in my power to make my dream of becoming a jockey a reality. By the time I am fourteen years old, I enroll in an adult horse husbandry class in Old Westbury, New York, that is held twice a week for twelve weeks. I ask my father if he will drive me to the North Shore of Long Island, and he says, "Yes, of course."

There are a good number of people in the class ranging from my age to about sixty years old. The teacher is a horse trainer and he asks us why we are taking the course. When I say, "I want to become a jockey," everyone laughs at me, and I feel ashamed.

I am learning a lot in class: six weeks of studying about horses and their possible diseases, then six weeks of working hands on with the horses. The teacher says to me, "If you are serious about becoming a jockey, you should take riding lessons." I am given a name of a riding teacher, and I call and book my first lesson. It feels great learning how to ride the English saddle.

I am paying for the instructions with money I earn myself, as I learned very early on that if I wanted anything, I needed to work for it. I gain horse knowledge and skills from my class, and every weekend I go to work on a horse farm on the North Shore. The North Shore of Long Island is horse country.

My father is very supportive of my quest to become a rider. My mother is not, but as I've explained, we have a distorted relationship. Our association is very superficial, and based on a false persona, a fake personality in which I intuitively grab onto an illusion. I have this notion I will become a famous jockey, and people will admire me. At this point in my life, I am lifting my self-esteem by this grandiose delusion. My sense of personal value is like an aircraft that is cruising smoothly above for now, but will sooner or later run out of fuel and crash.

Chapter 11

Chris

I encounter a set of circumstances that will lead me to realize I'm a natural on a horse. My mother is pals with a man who works at a thoroughbred horse farm in Elloree, and this family friend brings me to meet the owner of the farm. Right away Mr. Smith, the owner, sees I am the right size to become a jockey.

Before I can get on a horse, my job is to muck out stalls and groom the horses. I go to the farm every day after school. I am falling in love with the thoroughbred. One day Mr. Smith finally puts me on a horse, and at this moment, the special gift I have been born with becomes immediately apparent: I've spent time on the ground with the majestic racehorse, but now I am able to connect with their inner essence from above.

As I am sitting high in the air, I feel I can kiss the sky. For a moment, I become part horse, and am devoid of any fear. I can feel their heartbeat and see the spark of life from their breath. I make the connection, as we are one. Horses know I have a deep communication with them, for I can sense their immortal being.

I am becoming the star rider. Every spring the farm sets up what they call the Elloree trails, a day of races for their horses to compete in. I ride four horses and come in second in my first race. What do you think happened on my other mounts? I win, of course.

I'm enthralled when I realize that in the Arabian desert, the sound of the *zaghareet* (a high-pitched howl) celebrates the heart and soul of this animal. I have chills running up and down my spine knowing my inner bond with their spiritual being has given me the ability to be a natural rider.

I know horses are an escape for me. I am living in a broken home, and my father lives apart from my family. My mother is overpowering, and doesn't give me her emotional support. She is focused on my siblings' needs, and is distraught over the divorce. Where is my anger? Have I expressed my hurt? Mr. Smith considers me a son, and says my mom and dad split up just before I came to him. He says I was looking for something to grab onto, so I started with horses.[1]

Here I am focusing on my passion, the love of riding racehorses. When do I have the time or knowledge to understand what the most important things are in life? I am passive and caring by nature, the opposite of my mother. I fall into pleasing others, like most of us who are docile, and can't say "No."

Will I ever understand that I need to become an empowered person? Will I become a person who can make wise decisions in life? Will I ever have emotional security? I feel powerful on a horse, and will prove that I can squeeze in between horses and shoot through that tight space to win a race. Will I prove to have a plan to develop myself as well?

For the summer of my sixteenth year, I'm going to Atlantic City, New Jersey. Mr. Smith is sending me to the Garden State to gallop horses for his brother. The track in Atlantic City is enveloped with swirling mist from the early morning dew. I feel I can part the fog by running my horse right through this hazy veil. I love it, and it feels great to me. I am so focused on becoming a jockey, and people can see I am a natural.

I am growing up fast, and I know it. I notice people around me using drugs—will I have the power within to refuse them? The drugs look enticing, but I really don't care. I just want to ride racehorses!

The summer's warmth is leaving, and heading towards the southern hemisphere, and I'm now home in Carolina. For the next year, I will be going to school, and working and riding at the horse farm. I am watching cowboy movies to learn what they are doing on a horse. I am also viewing videos of past and present races, to understand what the role of a jockey is all about.

Will I set myself up to be one of the greatest jockeys who ever lived? I quit school in my junior year after going to the prom with a girl who asked me to accompany her to the party. My parents are not too happy about my decision to leave school. I tell my father that I'll be making ten thousand dollars a year. Little did I know at the time, I will be making ten thousand dollars a week!

I have an offer to ride in races in Maryland during my seventeenth year on this planet. I am also a people pleasing, disempowered, blue-green-eyed country boy. I'll be entering a world where I'll encounter temptations—will I be able to handle them?

Chapter 12

Serena

Chris Antley is galloping horses at Atlantic City racetrack in the summer of 1982. I am in Saratoga Springs that same summer, working for trainer John Parisella.

I am surprised my controlling mother is permitting me to go to Saratoga for four weeks, but working is approved of in my household, and having a social life isn't. If I asked her whether I could go to Saratoga with my friends, she would not have allowed it.

My parents and I are on the New York State thruway, making the three and a half hour drive from Long Island to Saratoga Springs. I am a little apprehensive about leaving home for the first time, but then I thought, it's only four weeks.

Saratoga Springs is an old village nestled in the Adirondack Mountains of New York. The town is centered on the oldest racetrack in the United States. Beautiful Saratoga is also home to horse racing's Hall of Fame.

In the year 1777, The Battle of Saratoga, a major battle in the American Revolutionary War, was fought in the town of Stillwater. General John Burgoyne, leader of the British army, surrendered to General Horatio Gates, the head officer of the American soldiers. This victory for the Americans gained the respect of their allies, and the American quest for independence was won.

A quick fifteen-minute drive from the site of the Battle of Saratoga brings you to the resplendent Saratoga Lake. The lake is quaint and picturesque, with houses lining the road, overlooking the body of water. I am renting a house on the lake with a few people. It has four bedrooms and an attic that I'm sharing with a friend I met working on the farm on Long Island.

My parents and I say good-bye, and I feel my anxiety leaving me little by little. I settle into the lake house, and start to make friends. I don't drive yet, so my friend from Long Island drives me to the racetrack where I will be working. A couple of days pass as I am connecting with people and working hard. I already love Saratoga and its dynamic environment.

Back in the early to mid-1900s, Saratoga saw the likes of the Vanderbilts, the Whitneys, J.P. Morgan, and actress Lillian Russell with her partner Diamond Jim Brady. The singer Bing Crosby sold out to packed audiences as he performed in the downtown hotels. Saratoga was and is the place to be!

Chapter 13

Serena

When horse racing arrives in Saratoga Springs for the month of August, the village transforms into a colorful, classic, exciting place. Every morning the horses go out on the track for their morning gallops. When they come back to the barn, I cool one of those horses down by walking them around the shed row (a dirt path around the barn) for thirty minutes. The day starts at 5:30 a.m. and ends around 11:00 a.m. If a horse is running in a race, I have to walk them after the race, but that doesn't happen every day. John Parisella tells me he has a daughter my age; one afternoon at the barn, we briefly cross paths. Twenty-five years from now, best-selling author, entrepreneur, and reality-show-star Bethenny Frankel *(*her biological father is the Hall of Fame horse trainer Bobby Frankel*)* will be well known.

At night, a group of us go to house parties in town and on the lake. There's a nightclub that's particularly trendy, filled with people drinking and dancing. Called the Rafters, the disco with its huge dance floor is built on a hill with a wraparound deck overlooking Saratoga Lake. Inside a fog machine makes this place magical with its laser lights, along with three bars, and winding staircases. I am sixteen years old, and the legal drinking age at the time is eighteen, so I barely make it inside with my fake identification card.

I do make it into the club, and I'm wowed by the likes of the horse trainers, owners, and jockeys that I see, such as the awesome Hall of Famer Angel Cordero Jr., one of the greatest jockeys of all time. I am just having fun, having a drink and dancing all night.

Two weeks have passed, and I feel elated that I am in such an electrifying and special place as Saratoga. My parents are coming to visit me this weekend, and I'm thrilled. I am going to tell them what an amazing time I have been having.

Saturday afternoon is here, and I am strutting along Union Avenue, about to enter the main gate of Saratoga racecourse. I hear a young boy around nine years old yelling, "Get your *Daily Racing Forms* here!" Horses are being led by their grooms and crossing the busy street. They are taking the path to the paddock, which runs through the area.

It is a beautiful, sunny, warm day, and it's thirty minutes until post time. I see my parents relaxing by a picnic table eating lunch and say, "Hi Mom and Dad! I'm having a fantastic time here, working during the day and going out at night."

"How could you do that?" my mother yells at me. "You know we don't do those things." I'm feeling so ashamed; here again, I am doing something wrong, and instinctively I withdraw into my familiar shell.

This is one of many mommy-envies. My mother is envious that I'm having fun. It feels shameful to me that my own mother is envious of her own daughter: it says that I'm worthless, and she is the superior one. She is resentful and then criticizes me—this way she feels grand and props up her self-esteem. Where is my self-esteem in all of this? It is nowhere to be found.

My parents leave late Sunday, but I still have one more week in Saratoga. I have been hanging out with a guy I like, and we are having a wonderful time. We are kissing, but that is the extent of the sexual encounter. The week is going fast, and I hitch a ride back to Long Island with a friend I am rooming with.

I'm back home and I say, "Mom, Dad, I have a boyfriend! Isn't that smashing?" My parents are silent, and don't say anything until a day later. I see my boyfriend later that day and he breaks up with me. I am devastated, crying my eyes out in my room, while my mother is in a rage.

"Are you doing it in the back seat of a car, you whore? You goddamned son-of-a-bitch," she is yelling. "I told your father I should have never sent you to that goddamned racetrack. I always said you are no goddamned good. You are going to be the death of me. You better just change your ways, or get the hell out."

My heart is broken and my mother is the big “B.” She has absolutely no empathy. Tragically, she doesn’t care how I feel. She just wants to control me.

Chapter 14

Serena

Summer is over, and school is starting again. I will be getting school credit for working in the mornings at Belmont Park. I have decided to graduate a year early, so I'm taking night classes. Ten months go by in a blink of an eye, and June is upon us. I've just graduated high school, and in January I'm going to Virginia. My boss in New York is affiliated with a horse trainer in the southern state. I'm going to the horse trainer's farm to become a professional rider of racehorses!

Of course my mother is giving me the guilt trip that I shouldn't be leaving her, but at this point I can't internalize her guilt. I know the one thing I want is to become a jockey. It's January and it's cold, and my father and mother, and aunt and uncle are driving me to Virginia. The State of Virginia is gorgeous, and I will be living in a very small town called Free Union, about thirty minutes from Charlottesville.

I will give myself two years here to learn the technique of riding racehorses. At first Felix, the owner of the horse farm, didn't put me on a horse. After a couple of weeks he did, and he saw I knew the basics of riding. Now, I am galloping horses on the track and working in the stables grooming the yearlings. As time goes on, I know I don't have the confidence to be a good rider. I'm not great balancing myself on top of a horse and keep falling off, but I have the resilience to stick with it. However, I've recreated a scenario in which Felix is very much like my mother. Felix is a domineering man, and I am afraid of him. I am so fearful I might make a mistake that I keep making errors. I can't build up my self-assurance with someone constantly yelling at me not to make a misstep.

One day I am galloping a colt and Ginny, the girl who is the star rider, starts shouting at me, "Come on, you have to keep the horses head to head." I didn't say anything, but I should have said, "I'm trying, and it isn't working." So the girl screams at me for not keeping up with her. "You bitch," and she goes ahead of me on her horse. I should have spoken up for myself but I didn't.

We finish our gallop and head back to the barn. Ginny is telling the owner what happened. I overhear Felix say to Ginny, "She probably deserved you yelling at her." I feel ashamed and I go into my shell.

I'm in Virginia a year and decide I've had enough of riding, and people treating me with disrespect. Felix convinces me to stay, saying he thinks I can be a good rider. *That is just hogwash—he's looking out for himself, because he knows I am a hard worker. He's exploiting me for his own reasons, just like my mother uses me to meet her own needs.*

One frosty morning I nonchalantly stroll to one of the enclosed areas where a chestnut colt is grazing. His time is up outside, and he needs to be put in his stall. I open the gate and approach him, and without warning the colt lunges at me. He is all pumped up and aggressive, testosterone pouring out of him. His mouth is wide open and he bares his teeth to bite me. Suddenly those menacing teeth rip my T-shirt and take a bite into my skin, just below my right breast. I am shocked to see that blood is everywhere, and I think he has chopped my breast right off, but thank God he didn't touch my chest. I stand there for about five minutes, bruised, bloody, and in pain. Then I go over to him again, put the lead shank on his nose, and bring him into the barn. My wound heals after a couple of weeks, but I will have a faint scar on my body for the rest of my life.

Months go by and I am galloping a young dark brown filly around the track. Ginny is screaming at me again to keep up with her horse. I'm trying my best, and she continues to put me down. All of a sudden, my horse bucks her hind legs so high in the air that I hit the ground hard, falling on my left side. In 1985, the biggest liquor company is Seagram's and its owner, Mrs. Bronfman, is watching one of her horses gallop when I happen to fall.

I am lying on the dirt in agony, but I have pride and pick myself up. Pain is ripping through my whole body, and I can't stand upright, but I manage to walk off the racetrack. Mrs.

Bronfman sees me and puts me in her car, and we drive to the doctor's office, about twenty minutes away. I sit in the car, attempting to cope with the distress, but I ask her, "How much longer?"

She says, "We are almost there," and I burst out crying.

When we enter the doctor's office, and he sees what excruciating pain I am suffering, he drugs me right away. He takes x-rays, and says I have a dislocated shoulder, and he proceeds to put my shoulder back in place. I am so numb from the drugs that I don't feel any discomfort when he twists my arm back into its socket, but I'm relieved, as my arm feels so much better. Now I'm being released from the doctor's, and Mrs. Bronfman drives me to her summerhouse.

I can't believe my eyes—is it the drugs, I wonder? We are driving up a long driveway dotted with cherry trees. I take one look at her house, and realize this is not merely a house: it is a mansion. She parks her Mercedes-Benz on her massive driveway, and calls two of her housekeepers, who take me inside the castle, and carry me up a circular staircase.

The housekeepers guide me into a French country-decorated room. They proceed to undress me and put me in a warm bath. After the bath, they wrap me in a robe and lay me down on a bed. I am so intoxicated, I fall right to sleep; a few hours later, I wake up, and the housekeepers bring me some chicken and potatoes, with a piece of cake for dessert. A couple of hours after that, they bring me a hot cup of milk, and I sleep like a baby. I am at the chateau for two days, and everyone treats me with respect.

I meet Mr. Bronfman and two of his cousins. They have compassion for the terrible suffering I've gone through, falling off a horse and dislocating my shoulder. It's time to leave the dream. The Bronfmans pay for my plane ticket to fly home to New York, which is so very generous of them. It is a breathtaking experience—for a few days, I am treated like a queen.

I can't grasp the idea that I deserve the royal treatment. I am so used to being the servant of my mother and sisters that I can't grasp the concept of princess. That is exactly what I will need to learn in the future. Will I be able to make the transition from servant to empress?

Chapter 15

Serena

I fly home to New York for a couple of weeks to rest. While I am here I make a bold move: I decide I want a dog. I look in the newspaper, and I see a collie for sale. I have always wanted a collie, so my father and I drive forty minutes to Suffolk County on Long Island. We drive up to the house, and the dog is hanging out in the front yard on a leash, but I don't connect with the dog, so we leave.

My father says, "Let's go to this dog shelter up the block."

"OK," I say. We walk into the depressing refuge, and I spot a beautiful, one-year-old, red-and-white collie. I open his cage and start petting him, and I just know we belong together. I adopt him right away, as he would have been euthanized in the next three days if I didn't come and rescue him. I name my new friend Romeo, after Rosie's Romeo, a cute chestnut horse at the farm.

We sign all the paperwork, and I bring him to Virginia with me. I'm grateful to be able to create a bond with my new dog. He just loves to run around in the open fields behind the house where I live. The four-bedroom house I share with a couple of people I work with is in the woods, just half a mile from the training complex.

A couple of weeks go by as I examine my experience after my riding accident. I know that I'm not a natural rider, and I don't have the confidence I should have, but I don't want to admit my failure just yet. My boyfriend Peter wants to become a jockey too. He and I are talking about my future, and we agree I should leave Virginia to pursue riding in Florida. I really want to live in a climate where the sun shines most days, and it's warm all year round. I have spent two years in Virginia, and I decide to move at the end of the year, but I don't have a solid plan for what to do next.

So I hobble back to New York, and to Mommy Dearest. In all the time I am in Virginia, my mother burdens me with a guilt trip, saying she doesn't have long to live and I should come home, but I don't pay attention to what she's saying, because I'm focused on my goal. Now I'm going home, and really don't have a blueprint for what I should do next. Peter and I pack my belongings, and we make the drive from Virginia to New York.

I know I don't want to stay with my mother, and decide I should go to Florida. Before I go, I'm in New York for the interim. Now that I am here, my mother senses she has control over me again. She hates Peter, and does everything in her power to prevent me from seeing him.

My mother throws herself on the floor, and pretends to have a heart attack. My sister says to me, "See what you have done," to which my father responds in a nasty tone, "Let her go."

Furious, I reply, "I am twenty years old, and I am just going out for the night with my boyfriend!"

Peter goes back to Virginia for another couple of months. My father says, "Do you think that he is going to be thinking about you?" I'm getting shot down everywhere I turn. Will I ever recover and pull through life? I have low self-worth. I simply don't feel safe or secure. I lack personal power, and my dog is the only pleasure in my life.

Without my dog, my father accompanies me to the Sunshine State. We are both probably thinking we want a break from the winter, but also from my mother. We hop into my father's Pontiac, and share the drive down Interstate 95. We drive about twelve hours the first day and stay in a motel in St. Augustine, Florida, that night. The next day we arrive in Hollywood, Florida, and go to the races at Gulfstream Park. I see a guy I know at the races, and he tells me my boss in Virginia should have recommended me to a trainer. I don't have any connections here that will help me find a job and ride, so my father and I decide it is best to go back to New York, and after a week in the warmth we head up north.

Now, I really don't know what to do. I venture back to Belmont Park for the time being and groom horses. Meanwhile, Peter is leaving Virginia as he has a link in Hershey, Pennsylvania, to ride. Right at this moment, I hear a friend of mine is looking for a rider at Garden State Racetrack in Cherry Hill, New Jersey. I drive to New Jersey and get on a couple of horses, but it doesn't work out, so I leave there after a week. Chris Antley is the leading rider at Garden State right now, but I don't know that at this point. In fact I don't even know of Chris Antley at all.

I don't know what else to do, so I follow Peter to Pennsylvania, thinking that it might lead to an opening to ride. One day I'm hanging out with Peter, his brother, and sister-in-law. They are doing cocaine, and I try it for the first time, but the drug doesn't do anything for me. I don't experience any unbelievable feeling from it, and I never try the drug again.

Meanwhile, I still don't have any confidence in myself to ride. I am holding on to the illusion that I will gain admiration. My unmet essential childhood need is controlling my life. My self-worth is on a plane, and the aircraft is running out of fuel and will crash very soon.

While I'm in Pennsylvania, Peter and I start to have problems. Emotionally I'm a mess, and I let myself become vulnerable. He is on his way to becoming a jockey, and he is going to ride and win his first race next week. He has become cocky and controlling, and is taking advantage of me. I feel my confidence plunging lower and lower: the plane is going to hit the ground any minute now.

Peter and I are breaking up, and it is incredibly tough on me—I am crying with such intensity you could probably hear me across the Atlantic. I don't want him to leave and am screaming hysterically, tears rolling down my cheeks, "Please don't leave me! Please don't leave me!" He does leave, and I feel myself reenacting my childhood. My mother left me emotionally. Now when a boyfriend leaves, I feel like my entire security is being destroyed, and like I will not survive.

I do have a job, and I hang around Pennsylvania for the time being. I am staying at a friend's, and to get my mind off of things, I enter a gym. One of the people at the gym says to me, "You have great concentration when you work out." That is all I need to hear, and that is what starts me on my fitness quest.

As Peter broke up with me, and I am not riding here, I feel I've had enough of Pennsylvania, and I make the painful decision to limp home. I know it sounds crazy, but since I lost the feeling of safety with my boyfriend, I need to find that security somewhere else. What I have not yet discovered is that this sense of protection has to come from within.

However, at this point in my life, the only way I know how to seek that care is to go home to New York and deal with Mommy Dearest. Like a small infant I am running back to Mommy to try to get her love and approval. It is September of 1986, and I am completely miserable, lost, and vacant. The plane has just crashed. Are there any survivors? I have survived but am in critical condition, barely alive.

Chapter 16

Chris

I am on my way to becoming an amazing jockey. Maryland is welcoming me as I win my first race on June 11, 1983. As soon as I jump off my horse, I know what's going to happen. I skip into the jocks room, turn my head, and boom, I'm hit with shaving cream, water, anything the other jockeys can throw at me. Oh my God, I'm drenched! I can't see, but I'm not considered a maiden anymore (a horse or rider who has never won a race).

I'm just starting to gain my confidence now. Do I really have self-assurance? Sure, I have faith in myself as a rider. As a person, on the other hand, I act like I'm arrogant, but that's just a cover-up—in truth, I don't have much self-esteem. I'm seventeen and growing up really fast, just like the main character in the movie *Big.* In the film, actor Tom Hanks plays a twelve-year-old kid who one day wishes to be a grown up; his wish is granted, and suddenly he finds himself in a grown man's body. Only then does he realize he never got to be a teenager, and decides he wants to return to being a kid.

I finish out the year in Maryland, and I'm getting better with each race I ride. I have made connections with trainers in New Jersey, and for the new year, I decide to make the move from Maryland to the Jersey circuit. I've been working with an agent I met in Maryland who has been having personal issues and just quit handling my book, so now I need someone new to represent me.

New Jersey is where I meet my dear friend Drew, a suave talker and the greatest agent I will have. Together, we'll blow away most of the other jockeys and their agents in New Jersey. With his striking, dark brown hair and great smile, Drew says to people, "Chris has the eyes and face of an angel."[v] I never knew that he gave me such a profound compliment—I guess he can sense I know things intuitively that others cannot grasp. Maybe

Drew is able to look deep inside me and perceive my eternal spiritual essence? He knows I have a gift that God gave me, and later says that I was unbelievable on horseback, that it was surreal to watch, almost as if I were part horse.[vi]

I become the leading rider, with a total of 849 races. I win 171 of those races in 110 days, a record I believe, which still stands seventeen years later. I win $665,991 and I get ten percent; my agent gets a percentage, and my personal jockey valet gets a small cut as well. I'm getting a lot of praise, but does that fulfill me? The answer is no. Drew calls me one of the most beautiful people in this world.[vii] Do I believe that about myself? The answer is no.

I'm starting to drink socially, and if I'm at a party or social gathering, I'll drink a beer. Back at the racetrack, I'm smashing records, and I'm not an apprentice rider anymore. I am a fully-fledged journeyman rider, winning consecutive riding titles. I am now known as the *Ant*.

I'm making sixteen thousand to twenty thousand dollars a week. For the year, I will make $2,741,736 in purse money. Deep down, do I believe I deserve to be making all this money? The answer is no. I am starting to smoke pot now—it's not a problem, or at least, I don't see it as one.

On the racetrack, I am a fierce competitor, and my fellow jockey friends know it. The electricity that radiates from my hands as I'm pumping my horse down the stretch creates magic. I cross the wire first 469 times in 1985, making me the leading rider in the United States. I make $5,968,806 in purse money for the year. I'm so thrilled, but what does it mean? I have so much money, but I don't have an identity. I don't have self worth. I don't have an appreciation for the things around me.[viii] I am lost, and I don't know how to fix it.

Sure other people have a high opinion about me, but I don't admire myself. I have a lot of emotions inside of me, and I don't know where to begin to get in touch with them. So I will continue to cover up my emotions with outside substances. Drew tells me, "Chris, the only time I see you in control is when you're on top of a horse, the fifteen minutes from when you board a horse in the paddock, to the time a race is over."[ix]

I don't have a clue how to understand myself. I put on a mask, but deep down I'm so shy and insecure. My friends are using cocaine, and I start to be very curious about this mysterious white substance. I have the money to afford such a luxury, right?

I am having a lot of people at my house tonight to watch the races. My friends are sitting at the table, and I see the white stuff on the table. I look at it and am curious about it, but walk away still thinking to myself, what are they doing? My friends walk out of the room. I get up and touch the white stuff. I taste it. When I sit down, I notice my tongue is numb, and then I snort it. I don't think it does anything at first, and I don't like it, but soon after that night I try it again, and change my mind.[x] I still think that I'm using this white stuff for social reasons. Here I am, a young kid making so much money, and now I have the pleasure of socializing while high on cocaine.

Spring is here, and we are at Garden State racetrack, and I'm the leading rider. On the racetrack, I am winning left and right. Fear doesn't enter my mind, as my spiritual gift is bringing me tons and tons of money. Months later the jet-set life is immersing me in a splashy existence, as I ride at Monmouth Park by day. Then at dusk I hop on a helicopter with another jockey to ride at night at Atlantic City Racetrack.

Making my riding weight at 110 pounds is not a problem, and on most days I cross the wire first multiple times. Drew and I are thinking about hitting the big city, and we head to New York. California and New York are two of the top states where the best of the best horses, trainers, and jockeys are competing.

It's September of 1986, and I am looking forward to riding in New York. Watch out New York, because Chris Antley is coming! If I can make it there, I can make it anywhere!

Chapter 17

Serena

I have just moved home with Mommy Dearest. I am so miserable; I'm twenty years old, and feel like a failure. My boyfriend broke up with me, and now I'm living with my controlling mother again. My father is also in the house, along with my sister, Fran.

I don't know what I want to do; I really don't want to groom horses for the rest of my life. I'm abandoning my grandiose delusion of being admired. My self-worth was based upon an illusion, and now there is nothing solid to hold me up. I am sinking in quicksand, and the deeper I submerge, the harder it is to survive.

What is keeping me going is my dog, and I transfer my gym membership from Pennsylvania to New York, so I'm working out on a consistent basis. I start hanging out with some people from the gym, and my mother is throwing a tizzy, yelling at me, "You need to stop socializing, and get a job."

Within a couple of days, I drive to Belmont Park and apply for a job grooming horses. I feel like a failure, and I want to hide. I am grooming for a claiming trainer, and his barn is located in what the backstretch of the racetrack calls the hole. About five barns are in this area, and the trainers who inhabit them, in my opinion, are low-class.

The son of the owner of the farm in Virginia is a jockey here now. I do not want to run into him, so being down here is an escape for me. I still want to try and ride, and my new boss puts me on a few horses, but it doesn't work out. At this point, I completely give up the idea of riding. Yes, I'm sabotaging myself. I'm giving up, because what is the use anyway? For the next year, working out is my crutch. I become addicted to exercise. I don't want to feel, and I am numbing myself through working on my body.

I am now fully caged, like an animal at the zoo, and my controlling, domineering mother has the key to the cage. She is the master and I am her slave, and I can't socialize. So to keep my sanity, I form relationships with the opposite sex based upon one-night stands. This is the only way I know how to have a little peace of mind.

My belief is I am not worthy of a relationship so I have hidden sex encounters with men at different times. Some of these encounters are great, others not so great, but I am being admired for my body, getting the praise I am looking for. Although I'm admired by all, I am loved by none. That is what I feel I deserve.

At work I am taking care of horses, and I hate it; I'm working for a man who degrades me. He says I don't work right, and tells me, "Men look at you, because you dress too provocatively." I am wearing leggings with a tee-shirt over them. It is not a good situation that I am in; people are dishonoring me, and walking all over me, and I just let it happen. My head has been so filled with messages that I am not worthy, that I am bad, that I just feel empty and lonely.

Chapter 18

Chris

Here I am making a brand new start in the Empire State—at Belmont Park! There are so many great riders competing for mounts. I do have the confidence that I will ride great. Drew is working day and night, securing me rides on the best horses. Drew and I are a team, creating lasting connections with the top owners and trainers. But am I happy? I appear to be: I am making tons of money, and I drive an eighty-thousand-dollar white Mercedes-Benz.

I am only twenty years old, and I have all the material things that should make me satisfied. Sure I have money, and money is fine to help you get by, but it doesn't make you happy. It doesn't give you love in your heart every day.[xi] Where is my sense of self? Am I in touch with my anger? Where is my mother? Where is my father?

Coming from a chaotic household, I left too early, and I didn't establish a solid sense of self or a strong emotional foundation within. I'm living in a lonely world. Yet I have a mental ability other people do not: I am able to sense the intangible. A few years ago horses were my escape; now I am starting to numb myself with alcohol.

I just failed a Breathalyzer test at the Meadowlands racetrack, as I was drinking beer at a Rutgers-Florida college football game in New Jersey. After I fail the test, Drew later remembered thinking to himself, *that was probably the first tip-off,*[xii] meaning that I was not going down the right track. Yet I am working hard, riding races in New York by day, then hopping in Drew's car and driving forty-five minutes on the New Jersey Turnpike to ride at the Meadowlands at night.

It is Monday the 16th, a sweet November afternoon, and I'm set to ride a filly named Majeboo at Aqueduct. We are in the gate, and we are off and running. On the top of the stretch we take the lead and win the $31,000 Mommy Dearest purse by three-quarters of a length, and set a track record.[xiii]

This is the 1980s. Hair-metal bands are rocking on the radio, and the U.S. economy is booming. People are making money, and partying all night long. I am starting now to use cocaine more, getting to the point where I do a lot. I remember one time when I did cocaine four out of six days—not all in a row —but I had picked it up, and used it. I got so weak, and I guess what I did was bottom out.[xiv]

I suppose I am looking for something outside of myself to lift my self-esteem. I have the praise, but it does nothing for my own sense of self. I have a fragile emotional ego and I lack confidence in my feelings and in my desires and wishes. A friend of mine sensed that a couple of years ago.

I would tell him about all the girls I was seeing. My friend said all I ever talked about was, "Oh, I met this one. This one is pretty, and I was with her." My friend knew I was lying. He knew I never had any of it. He knew it was a fantasy of mine because if it weren't, I would have latched. My friend sensed it had to be an ego buildup. I would tell him I was with the prettiest little girl last night, but when he'd ask me, "How come no one saw you? Why didn't you show up at the party?"[xv] I couldn't give him an answer.

My personality tells me I should not be using drugs, but my emotions want to numb the pain. I don't have the power within to make a wise choice. The temptation of this simple fix is not easy to resist. My ability to have good judgment about what I choose will haunt me about every important decision I will make, whether it's regarding drugs or whom to love for the rest of my life.

Chapter 19

Serena

After a year of being caged in my parents' house, I am utterly lost. I find solace by working out six days a week, and am going to enter a bodybuilding competition in a couple of months.

Regarding my work situation, I just left my job after a year of being trampled upon and belittled by my boss. Now I am grooming horses for trainer Nick Zito. Working with racehorses is like being a servant to them. Your job is to take care of them, make their bed, clean them and make sure they don't get hurt. This is the perfect place for me, since I am the best at thinking and caring about my mother. The whole purpose in taking care of racehorses is for them to win races.

It's now Friday, November 20, 1987. I have to take my brown horse, Tell It Honestly, on a disgusting thirty-minute ride in a cold van from Belmont Park in Elmont, to Aqueduct Racetrack in Ozone Park. I have time to go home before I get on the truck. I drive to Oceanside, and quickly change clothes, and grab a pair of thinly lined gloves.

I am now in the barn area of Aqueduct. It is cold and nasty, and the barn is repulsive, with pigeons shitting everywhere. It is time for Tell It Honestly and me to get ready for his race. I slip his bridle on, and we take the fifteen-minute walk to the paddock area. (The paddock is where the horses get saddled for the race.)

The winds of Jamaica Bay are alarming and distressing, and the frigid air is ripping through my gloves. Little by little the blood flowing through my hands halts. I am not wearing suitable clothing for a cold, sunny autumn day. It feels like winter in Queens, New York.

The misery I am feeling is unbearable, and I'm crying like a baby. When I get to the paddock, the assistant trainer Scotty asks me, "What's wrong?" I say through my tears that my hands are hurting, so Scotty takes Tell It Honestly from me and says, "Go inside and get warm."

I say, "OK," and run into the grandstand of the racetrack, crying hysterically. As I enter the bathroom, I am filled with frustration, and I let my anger out by punching the wall and screaming, "I hate this."

After I vent my emotions, I run warm water on my hands so they can come alive again. My father is at the races, and he has brought me a sandwich from home, but I say, "I just want hot tea." My father buys me a cup so I can feel better. I am in a state of bafflement. I do not witness my horse being saddled, so I do not see the jockey who is going to ride Tell It Honestly.

Needless to say, Tell It Honestly runs his race and does not come in first, second or third. After my horse runs poorly, I see Scotty in the paddock, and he says, "I'll get the horse, just go back to the barn, and set up a bath for him."

I say, "Are you sure?"

He answers, "Yes." Then he continues, "Everyone asked me, what did I do to you? I told them that you were in pain."

I walk back to the barn, and I never see the rider get on or off Tell It Honestly. At this moment in time, I am not aware of this—but Chris Antley rode my horse!

Chapter 20

Chris

On the day when the veil lifts, and we can speak to heaven, I become the first jockey ever to win nine races in one day. Is my immortal being tapping into the abundance of the universe? I don't know, but I feel an invisible force helps me as I guide home four winners at Aqueduct in New York; a couple of weeks ago. On that chilly Halloween night, I also have five winners at the Meadowlands in New Jersey.

I make the Guinness Book of World Records. "It is almost like a dream," I tell the press. Believe it or not, I didn't know what the record was until they announced it. I've been having bad luck—my car got hit last night—but everything sure turns around. After I win four in New York, I am flying at an all-time high. I just can't believe it. I want to thank all the horsemen that put me on horses tonight.[xvi]

I look over at Drew and say, "I did well today."[xvii]

Years later Drew says that he thinks this is the first time I believe I deserve my success.[xviii] For this brief moment, I feel I am worthy of my achievements.

I just set an unprecedented record for winning nine races in one day. It's almost the end of the year, and out of 1,965 mounts, I won 340 races, came in second 306 times, and third 244 times.

My total purse earnings for the year of 1987 are $8,650,613, of which I get ten percent. Not bad, but I still feel so empty inside, and don't have a secure base. I'm able to sense the intangible, but I can't express what I know. To top it all off, the drugs are starting to control my life.

Chapter 21

Serena

I know in my heart I don't want to spend the rest of my life grooming racehorses, so I decide to make a plan. Nick Zito is taking his horses to Florida for the winter, so I need to find another trainer to work for. I decide I am just going to work in the mornings, walking horses, and then in the afternoon, I'm going to find another job.

In the meantime, I enter a bodybuilding contest. I am training hard, working out with heavy weights. I am on a strict diet, to help me get down to my lowest body fat composition. It's the day of my contest, and surprisingly, my mother and father, my sister Fran, and a family friend are going to my contest! I look good on the day of the show, and have baby oil all over my tanned, pumped up body. I am very disappointed that my sister Mary Lou and my brother in law Steve are not here to support me.

I enter the lightweight category. The first round is where the all the contestants pose and show off their physiques, and it's at this stage that the winners are usually picked. The second round is in the evening, and the contestants pose to their routine. I come in third out of five people competing in my weight class. I am OK with the outcome, but of course I want to win, as I am still craving admiration. My mother and father think a bodybuilding competition is a little strange. They never see me compete again.

≈

Chapter 22

Chris

I set an amazing record for winning nine races in one day, but that was yesterday. If I want to stay in this game, I have to keep winning.

It is nonstop for me: I get up early, around 5:30 a.m., and I arrive at the barns ready to get up on a horse, and work them out. This is all I do, but I love it. "If I die, I want to die on the racetrack: it's my heart, it's my soul."[xix] It's my heart and soul, but do I really know my heart and soul?

I find working out gives me peace of mind. My fellow jockey friend Gary Stevens says about me that I have always been a workout fanatic—I look like a bodybuilder.[xx] From the strength working out gives me, to the knowledge when I read the racing form, every day I plot where my horses should be in any given race. I feel if I can jockey for a good position, whether I'm on a speed horse or a come-from-behind horse, I will have a better chance at winning. In the distant future *People* magazine will say that I am an intuitive, fearless rider with an almost mystical rapport with horses.[xxi]

A few weeks go by and one of my colleagues, jockey Robbie Davis introduces me to his sister. We hit it off, and now we are together as a couple. So now I have a girlfriend, and I am winning races left and right. Why don't I feel fulfilled? Winter is coming, and I will be riding races six days a week at Aqueduct. I express to Drew that I'd like to pick up some potential Kentucky Derby mounts.

≈

Chapter 23

Serena

I am very centered in knowing what I want, and I make a wise decision. Aqueduct Racetrack is off my radar, and I only want to work in the mornings at Belmont Park. I'll find another job in the afternoons until I decide what I'm going to do for the rest of my life. For a second, I am coming out of my servant-like mentality.

I am becoming empowered, and by voicing what I do not want to do, my ability to say no is enhanced. Since I am unconscious of what I am doing, this might be a short-lived moment. By the winter of 1988, I am working for D. Wayne Lukas. With his three-thousand-dollar suits and his porcelain laminates, Wayne Lukas is considered the Donald Trump of racing.

Jeff Lukas, Wayne's son, is training his father's horses here in New York, while Wayne trains his string in California. Jeff Lukas's assistant trainers, Kieran McLaughlin and Mark Henning, accommodate my request so I don't have to venture off to Aqueduct in the afternoon.

We all remember the tale of Cinderella, who was the youngest in her dysfunctional family. All of us only want to talk about the end result of this beautiful story. But Cinderella had to go through the depths of hell to get to her fairy tale result: Cinderella was abused by her stepmother and two stepsisters. I similarly take abuse from my mother and two sisters. And now I come out of my Cinderella existence for a second. What happened to Cinderella when she came out of her role? She met her prince.

Chapter 24

Chris

It's early in the year 1988, and I am looking for some Kentucky Derby prospects.

The alarm clock goes off practically in the middle of the night. It is a struggle to get up before dawn in the winter. It is so cold riding races six days a week, in January in New York. I wear a ski mask and gloves as I am riding in top form and I am one of the leading riders at the Aqueduct meet.

The New York Racing Board wants me to take a drug test: will I pass? I doubt that I will, and I don't know what will happen to my career if I test positive. Just like I feared, I don't pass the test. Neither the public nor the racing world knows about my testing positive at this time.

The New York State Racing and Wagering Board only needs "a reasonable cause" before the Board may ask a rider to take a drug test. Dominic Bologna, head of the program, describes their guidelines in these terms: "When we have reason to believe an individual is involved in illegal drugs, he or she will be tested."[xxii] There is reason to believe that about me, because just a couple of months ago, I tested positive for alcohol at Meadowlands Racetrack.

The program consists of 360 tests, and if 91 of those tests are positive, the Board will ask the person to withdraw from racing until further notice. That person will need to go into a program. If the Board then decides the person is capable, it will reinstate his or her license. If the person is compliant, then the racing board will take no further action.[xxiii] This is the program Drew and I adhere to.

Did I stick to it? Drew later remembers that I promise to never become involved with drugs again, but then I break my resolve.[xxiv] I say to myself, I can't smoke marijuana. Now, all that is left is alcohol, and drinking is a social thing.[xxv]

I am winning consistently two, three times a day. I'm going with the flow, as the money keeps rolling in. I think to myself, what if I'm suspended from riding? What would I do? I am grateful I am here right now. Does fate have anything to do with it, I wonder?

Chapter 25

Serena

As I hear a rooster crow signaling a start of a new day, I enter D. Wayne Lukas's barn. At first, it seems that this is just like any other day on the backstretch at Belmont Park. To keep me warm from this frosty environment, I am wearing layers of clothes. I sit on a bale of straw waiting for Dynaformer to come back from his morning gallop. Twenty minutes go by as I sip my coffee.

My horse is back from his daily exercise, and I am standing in front of this beautiful thoroughbred with his rider on top of him. His nostrils are blowing warm air into my face. The rider dismounts, and takes his tack with him. I grab a lead shank, and I put the chain around Dynaformer's nose and through his halter.

I take him outside for his bath. His groom splashes water on his body, scrapes the excess liquid off the big brown colt, and puts a blanket on him. I proceed to cool Dynaformer down by walking him around the shed row for thirty minutes. I am walking my horse for fifteen minutes or so while another set of horses are being saddled.

The next round of three or four horses going out on the track are going to be running their hearts out. They are preparing for a race, and will be galloping at full speed. Jockeys are called for this task frequently in the mornings, giving them a chance to get to know the horses before they ride them in a race.

All the forces of the universe are working together at this precise moment in time. I am strutting around the corner. Dynaformer and I are going stride for stride. I stop to let him drink some water. My horse and I are approaching the middle of the Shed Row. I can see my boss Kieran McLaughlin talking to an exercise rider. There are other people in the middle of the shed as well.

In fifteen years, Dynaformer will be a top stallion, siring the 2006 Kentucky Derby winner, Barbaro. Dynaformer and I are putting one step forward, and are now in the middle of the shed row. I turn my head to the left and…

Wow.

I take one glance at this gorgeous, extraordinary man. His sparkling, rich, luminous, emerald-green eyes exude astounding magic. This encounter produces in me an electrifying force that feels as if it were shooting out of my body. My immortal essence is merging with his eternal soul within seconds of this meeting, while the allure of this vibration penetrates deep within me.

I am utterly enthralled with the bliss of this sudden, harmonious melody fluttering throughout my entire being, as I feel myself being lifted up into a vibrant, glowing sphere of intense emotion. This radiant man has sent a profound love into the very core of my soul.

This powerful, vivid experience exists in time and space, but is transporting me beyond these dimensions as we know them. My heart is beating a mile a minute, and I am bewildered by him, as he is transfixed with me. We are in complete awe of one another. He feels enchanting and mystical to my six senses. His sensuous, delightful presence blows life into the sweet whispers of my divinely-inspired inner being. This heavenly sensation is sublime, reaching beyond human comprehension.

Chapter 26

Chris

On a cold February morning, I enter Wayne Lukas's barn.

I say, "Hi," to Mark, one of the assistant trainers to Jeff Lukas. He asks me how I am feeling, and I say, "I'm doing well."

He tells me that he has a filly for me to work; she will be running in a grade two stakes race next week. A grade one race is for star horses, and a step below that are horses running in a grade two. Mark asks me to work her three quarters of a mile, and see what she has for the last quarter.

I say, "OK."

Kieran comes over to say hi, and adds: "This is a great filly: if she performs well today she has a good chance of winning next week."

"Great," I say. "Let's see." I am in the middle of the shed row. Mark and Kieran are talking to an exercise rider. There are horses being cooled outside. I turn my head towards the shed row and…

Oh my God.

I take one look at this gorgeous, beautiful, enchanting, sensuous girl with free-flowing, sexy, long, dark brown hair. We are about the same height, inches away from each other, and I am floored. I know her—she exudes an otherworldly vibration, and we look intently at one other. I can feel the presence of a vault of heavenly stars shining upon her, a mysterious, supernatural light. Her captivating soul is putting me under a spell, and I can feel her rich, ethereal inner essence.

This extraordinary encounter makes me feel as if I have just arrived at a temple. I have been given access to the Divine. As I enter the room where the holy of holies resides, I can feel the spark of the Almighty deep within her. Her intense vibrant force makes me want to cry, and I am struck by the realization of how very close to her I am.

Chapter 27

Serena

I am both elated and mystified, having just experienced such an amazing moment. His eyes—oh my God—they are gorgeous. I have never seen eyes so green before. They just stand out, and you cannot help but be captivated by them.

Who is this guy? Is he an exercise rider? Is he a jockey? I don't know. Whoever he is just got up on his horse, and went to the main track to work the filly. I say to myself, I can't ask anyone who he is because they are going to think I'm interested. I can't like someone I am attracted to, as I'm not worth that much.

After so many years of suppressing my feelings, my soul is covered up behind a mask. My outer identity thinks I don't have the value to be loved. The depth of me cannot escape what I know or how I feel. I just put Dynaformer in his stall, and wait for another horse.

I grab the first horse that comes in the barn, and skip to the courtyard with him. The guy I was mesmerized by came back from the track, and left while I was outside. I still don't know who he is, and I'm wondering if I will ever see him again. I'm rethinking whether I should stay around the track for the time being. How can I leave after what I just encountered? I don't know it yet, but I am inching my way back towards the servant role.

A couple of days later the gorgeous guy is in the barn again. We see each other, and boom, he comes up to me, and stares into my eyes: I am wowed. I figure out, by the way he is talking to Mark, that he is Chris Antley, the jockey. Where have I been? I used to see Chris's name in the program, and I thought he was an old man. I never realized he would be my age, and that we could intuitively offer such sweet memories to each other. We are drawn together so vibrantly, like when an invisible force seductively draws attention to two magnets.

Chapter 28

Serena

Chris and I will see each other on average once or twice a week after our magical encounter. He comes into Wayne Lukas's barn early in the morning to work a few horses. We look intently at each other, just inches apart, and then we walk away. I do not fully understand what is going on.

My heart is electrified every time I see Chris. The mere fact of his presence stirs up a sense of rapture inside me. The feelings of bliss and exaltation are overpowering, and produce a trance-like state between us. I intuitively know I cannot leave the racetrack at this time. How can I? I am so happy—I'm full of ecstasy. I want to talk to him: why doesn't he want to talk to me?

My inner wisdom says we are connected, but I don't know how deep our bond really is at this point in time. To top it all off, my negative mind continues to pester me: *Why would he want to be with you? He is beyond your reach. He is a top jockey, and you are a stable hand. He is drop dead gorgeous, rich, and famous. You are struggling to find your own identity. Why would he want to talk to you?*

I am mesmerized and enchanted by his presence, but I fear I am not worth him loving me. *However, he is the one who comes up to me, and fixes his gaze upon me.* I am not making the first move. I do not go up to him. *It seems as if he is directed by a force within him, and then follows that lead. He feels drawn to come up to me, and look deeply into my eyes.*

≈

Chapter 29

Chris

It is bright and early as I venture to Wayne Lukas's stable.

As I enter Wayne's barn, I know I will see this pretty, surreal girl walking horses. She seems like she walked out of a painting, with her perfect hair and sculpted body, yet her essence is so overwhelmingly familiar.

My inner being is pulling me towards her, but I don't know what to say. I am not worthy of being loved at this deep place. I know she senses something. I have a feeling she knows me as I know her, but I don't feel confident enough to go up to her and say what I know. I am ecstatic, as if I am waking up out of my sleep to something very transcendent.

She feels mythical, so light and pure, as if somehow, in a distant past, we were so happy together, taking a walk in the clouds. I feel that this mysterious connection I have with a girl I don't know, is intuitively profound. I am bursting with energy every time I see her.

This energy leads me to a good place at this moment in time. Drew books me on an up-and-coming colt, a Kentucky Derby prospect. The horse's name is Private Terms, and I am going to ride him in a few weeks in a grade two stakes race.

≈

Chapter 30

Serena

Chris is being pulled towards me by a profound force. I am saturated with emptiness and hopelessness. I ache to be with Chris physically, but I don't fully understand. Our connection is so deep and profound. I am unable to comprehend the depth of our bond. I have a low sense of worth after all my years of not expressing my feelings—in short, I hate myself.

I can sense Chris sees me on a very intimate level, but I despise myself, and try to hide behind my addictions. Chris can see the real me, and that scares me—not to mention, I am concealing my life from my mother. Deep down, I know I can't have a relationship with Chris. My mother would infuse so much negative energy into it. I also know I would bring a lot of dysfunctional issues into the situation.

I know I do not deserve to be happy, but it feels rich just being in the same space as Chris, even if only for a few minutes, a couple of times a week. It's as if we can sense our heavenly hearts beating when our bodies are near each other. I am blown away by his abstract touch and I love the feel of his succulent essence penetrating deep within me.

≈

Chapter 31

Chris

Down the stretch I come! I, riding Private Terms, win the Gotham Stakes!

I think I just secured my first Kentucky Derby mount! His next race is the grade one Wood Memorial Stakes in a couple of weeks. He should win easily. Then, I am on my way to Louisville, Kentucky!

I am on a roll as a jockey, and it feels good. I know I can't use drugs at this juncture, so I keep drinking. I am just empty inside; life is meaningless to me. I am crossing paths with this girl who feels so imaginary. I feel we are in a dream when I see her. I am following my intuition, and I look directly into her eyes, and I know her. Sometimes I wonder, does she know me?

I also sense something is wrong with me. I wake up every morning, and the sun's not bright. I'm not excited to be a part of life. I don't want to get out of bed. I feel worthless.[xxvi] I hate myself, so how could she like me? It definitely takes a toll on one's mind and soul.[xxvii]

I feel unable to talk to the girl who puts me in a trance, but I can't ignore the force within me that keeps pulling me towards her. Yet I simply don't have enough personal strength to act upon what my intuition is telling me.

≈

Chapter 32

Serena

Chris asks the trumpeter to blow a lustrous noise to honor our link. I am on a high when Chris and I are in the holy presence of each other. My personality can never sustain this happiness. I'm a messed up, needy little girl in an adult body. I gave up on my dream to become a jockey. I am walking horses right now, and working as a waitress in a gourmet coffee shop.

The sad part about my condition is that I am not conscious of all my problems. I think Chris and I are going to be together, and all my troubles are going to be solved. We are going to live happily ever after. Deep down I know I am not worthy of love. My grandiose state of mind tells me I am going to be all right because of this spellbound interaction I have with Chris, but I am in a fantasy, thinking someone else is going to fill my unmet needs.

My pompous mind is setting me up for another crash, and when I do fall, I will fall into a deep depression. Where did my excessive aspiration for praise go? My undue need for admiration is still within me. What I don't understand is that my desire for approval is about not getting that primary requirement met as a child. An admired person is admired by all, loved by none.

I also want to be loved, and especially I want to be loved for who I am. I know Chris and I have an unusual intensity when it comes to our interaction with each other. We are drawn together, but I want him to fulfill my unmet needs. I intuitively know Chris sees the deeper part of me, but it is the shallow part that is so screwed up. For now I am daydreaming that I am going to be with Chris, and that all my problems will go away.

Chapter 33

Chris

I cross the wire first on Private Terms to win the Wood Memorial, a grade one prep race for the Kentucky Derby.

I am going to ride in my first Kentucky Derby, and I am overjoyed. It looks like we have a good chance in the most prestigious race in the sport. I am on a high. I worked hard to get here, and here I am. And I'm getting more pumped up every time I run into my heart-pounding, brown-eyed girl in Wayne Lukas's barn.

Somehow she feels so out of the ordinary to me. I just know we are linked. I can sense she sees the deeper part of me, but how can I connect with her at the verbal level? What do I say? Do I say, "Hey listen, I can see you, and I know you." First of all, I don't have the confidence to say that. She probably doesn't even like me. For now I am on my way to Kentucky, and I am going to win. It is exciting being in the thoroughbred capital of the world.

Everyone in the sport is preparing a horse for the most important race of the year. The Kentucky Derby is like the Super Bowl of horse racing. Horse people and the general public alike are interested in watching this beautiful race. I like my horse: he is undefeated in seven starts, and has an excellent shot at winning. I see people like him too, and he is the favorite to win.

I'm out on the track on this first Saturday in May. My horse and I are prancing in front of the famed twin spirals of Churchill Downs. I can faintly hear the famous song, "My Old Kentucky Home" playing in the background.

Private Terms is warming up great, and now we are approaching post time. We are in the starting gate, and before I know it we're off. My horse is five wide around the first turn, and I'm able to keep him in good position. I can see the second favorite, the filly Winning Colors. She is up front setting the pace.

I just don't have enough horse to push down the stretch with, and Winning Colors crosses the wire first.

My horse runs ninth, and gets defeated by six and a half lengths. The filly Winning Colors wins the 1988 Kentucky Derby. Winning Colors is ridden by Gary Stevens, and trained by Wayne Lukas—the same trainer the girl who mesmerizes me works for!

Chapter 34

Serena

The Kentucky Derby is upon us as May seventh arrives in the year 1988. Chris is riding in the race, and he has an honest shot at winning. My father places a bet on Private Terms to win.

I plop down on the couch in the den of my parents' house, and my father and I watch the Derby on our big television set. We are witnessing Winning Colors with Gary Stevens take the lead, and it looks like she is going to win. She is the second filly to win the Derby in a decade: Genuine Risk did it in 1980. The filly Regret won the race in 1915. Winning Colors is only the third filly to win the Derby in the history of the race.

My boss has just won the Kentucky Derby, and I didn't even bet on her. My father didn't have the winner, but he and I enjoyed the race. I'm up bright and early the next day, and everyone at my barn is jumping for joy. Work is the same as usual, as horses have to get out on the track for their daily workouts. The training and care for these horses is nonstop. So even though my barn won the Kentucky Derby, it does not slow the operation down. All the people I know who are involved in horse racing were either born into it, or have a passion for it. This is a seven-days-a-week, 365-days-a-year lifestyle.

≈

Chapter 35

Chris

Private Terms and I come out of the Derby unharmed. Two weeks pass, and now the 1988 Preakness Stakes is coming up.

Here I am in Baltimore, Maryland, at Pimlico Racetrack, getting ready for the second leg of the Triple Crown. I feel my horse Private Terms has a great shot in today's race. We just need a clean trip, and we can cross the wire first.

It is a cloudy but warm day with a huge crowd for today's race. I'm on the track, and I hear faintly the song "Maryland, My Maryland," being played in the background. It is post time!

My horse and I are in the starting gate, waiting for all the horses to enter. Before you can say, "Are we there yet?" we're off. My horse is lying well behind the leader, and we are in good stalking distance. Around the far turn I have hope, but I feel my horse doesn't have it in him to catch the leaders. We run fourth behind Risen Star, Brian's Time, and Winning Colors, the winner of the Kentucky Derby. My horse had no excuse. We just couldn't get there. I go back to New York, and I ride on Sunday at Belmont Park. Monday morning, I'm up at the break of dawn working horses.

As I enter Wayne Lukas's barn, I see her again, and wham. She is just beautiful. I just feel so drawn to this girl, and it feels like she is wearing a veil. Through this covering I can see it's the emergence of a new day. I can sense the mist of her being, rising out of the waters. Perceiving her vaporous energy is intoxicating, but my personality cannot act upon what I know to be true, so I just acknowledge her deep inner essence.

The next week I am riding a horse named Imanair. I clip heels with another horse in the race, and Imanair and I go down. My horse is OK, but I suffer a concussion, and will be out for a few weeks to recover. My fellow jockey friend Richard Migliore is not as lucky as I am. He was involved in the same spill. He suffers a dislocated spine, and will be out of commission for the next nine months.

For me, missing racing for a month will mean I won't be in the Belmont Stakes, but there has been talk that Private Terms will not run in the Belmont. Now I have a lot of free time on my hands. Will I be tempted to start using drugs again? The answer is probably yes, as I feel dead inside, and don't know how to stop.

Chapter 36

Serena

The cuckoo bird is chirping five times on this third Saturday in May. My father and I are intently watching the Preakness Stakes in the family room. It's twenty minutes until post time for the second gem of horse racing's Triple Crown. This very old, esteemed race is held in the state of Maryland.

My father places a bet on Winning Colors, the Kentucky Derby winner. Chris and Private Terms are third choice in the field. The horses are in the paddock, and the call comes for riders up. Horses and riders are led out onto the track. The song "Maryland, My Maryland," is playing, and it's ten minutes until post time. My father says to me his horse has a real shot at winning. I would like Winning Colors to win, but deep down I want Chris to be in front.

The horses are in the starting gate, and they're off. Forty-Niner goes to the front, with Winning Colors following close behind. Private Terms is fifth or sixth, on the backside of the racetrack. Down the stretch they come, and Risen Star takes command, with Brian's Time second, and Winning Colors third. Well, my father didn't win, Chris didn't win, and I didn't bet. I'm not much of a gambler. I just love to root for my horse, and watch the thrill of these magnificent creatures run.

Seven mornings later, in the barn area of Belmont, I see Chris. The diffuse mist of his energy creates an intensity of awe in and around me. Chris comes right up to me, just inches away. His exalted eyes have the allure of a sparkling emerald. If you wanted to purchase a precious stone that resembles his eyes, you could not acquire it on this earth. That is how rare his eyes and his inner essence are to this world.

A few weeks go by, and Chris is riding a horse named Imanair in the sixth race at Belmont Park. His horse's hooves come in contact with a horse in front of him, and Chris and Imanair hit the ground with extreme force. Imanair is OK, but Chris suffers a head injury. I send a basket of "Get Well" flowers to his hospital room, but I don't say whom the flowers are from.

Chris will not be riding for a few weeks. I, on the other hand, quit my job in the gourmet coffee shop, and return to the full time task of taking care of horses. I am in a different barn, working under trainer Jimmy Toner. I am back to grooming and going to the races in the afternoon at Belmont Park. Before I know it, I will be heading off to Saratoga Springs for the summer. I can't wait, as you know how much I love Saratoga!

Chapter 37

Chris

I'm out of racing for several weeks.

My addiction is not the cause of the spill. I did not use that week. After I go down and am recovering, I have a lot of time off, and pick up drugs again.

I'm too smart with the testing procedures, and how long the drugs stay in your system. I am going to be off a couple of more weeks, and if I use drugs now, it doesn't matter. I am not going to get tested, so I don't see it as a problem. I don't think it is any problem at all.[xxviii]

Drew is very concerned about me. He is worried that I am going to kill myself. He is anxious about where I am and what I'm doing. I am totally oblivious to his involvement—I just want to escape my pain. Weeks go by, and I am now fully recovered from my accident: I am back in the saddle again.

The July heat is here, and in a couple of weeks the racing circuit is going to Saratoga. Saratoga is a magical place to be. The atmosphere in Saratoga is uplifting and exhilarating. It just makes you want to freeze frame the moment in time. I pack my car, and in a few hours my girlfriend Kathy and I are heading up north on the New York State Thruway. We take pleasure in the ride, and before we know it, we're in Saratoga Springs.

≈

Chapter 38

Serena

The trees are as green as can be. I'm witnessing them from my car. It's summer. I feel alive, and I'm let out of my cage. The freedom I feel is fantastic. I'm driving north, heading to Saratoga. I make plans to rent an apartment with Maureen, a friend of mine. Eddie, a friend who works with me, is keeping me company for the drive. It's great having another person in the car; it makes the time fly by.

We make the three-and-a-half-hour trip in good time, and now we are approaching Saratoga. Thirty minutes north of Albany, Saratoga is a jewel in upstate New York. This diamond in the rough is an exit off the Northway, just three hours south of Montreal, Canada.

Saratoga consists of old Victorian houses that line the streets with their grandeur. The small but quaint hamlet is always thriving, with people strutting about. This is the place to be in the last two weeks of July and the month of August. The homes are filled with high society, who light up the racing season with elegant parties. Saratoga is just one big party!

The set of rooms I'm staying in is in the center of town, about five minutes from the racetrack. I drop off Eddie at his place, and settle in as Maureen arrives. This is the first night, and I am on a high. I go out on the town with Eddie, as Maureen decides to stay in. Eddie and I eat at Professor Moriarty's on the main street in downtown Saratoga, and when we finish dinner we decide to take a walk. Eddie and I are strolling on Broadway, when I look up and ten feet ahead of me is…

Chris and his girlfriend are wandering down Broadway, and Eddie and I are heading towards them. Chris makes a quick decision to cross the street. It is a smart choice, as soul is thicker than flesh. We would have created an awkward moment for the people with us. My heart is pumping a mile a minute, but I don't say anything to Eddie.

I go back to my apartment and tell Maureen what happened. I say, "I just ran into Chris. I was with someone, but he was with someone too, oh my God!" I forget what Maureen said. I am just so happy and elated. The next morning I wake up at 5:00 a.m. and head to work. I decide to stop at Dunkin' Donuts and get a cup of coffee and a donut.

I enter the Dunkin Donuts shop, and who is sitting at the counter eating a donut: Chris Antley. I walk in, and Chris jumps up and shouts to me, "Wow!" His immortal being is amazed, filled with wonder—the effect our souls have on one other is extraordinary.

My spirit is so thrilled at his enthusiasm, and I am leaping with excitement inside. Because I am so stunted at the spoken level, and have absolutely no self-value, I respond with just a smile. My soul is aching to be physically close to my everlasting mate. Chris and I are discovering the piercing vibration of our eternal existence, and it makes us scream with delight. Recognizing a soul whom I have loved for eons is a spine-tingling, pleasurable experience. The act of becoming consciously aware of our spiritual nature is an authentic, "Wow."

Chapter 39

Chris

I'm in Saratoga.

Kathy and I arrive at the gem of the Adirondacks Mountains, and it is fantastic to be here. I am going to be riding in tomorrow's races, but tonight Kathy and I are going out on the town. We just finished dinner, and decide to take a stroll on Broadway.

As we are taking a walk, I see her coming towards me—what do I do? I know if I strut by her I won't be able to control myself, as my heart-pounding girl will mesmerize me. I make a quick decision to cross the street; this way I will not create a blundering moment, and my girlfriend Kathy will not ask me any questions. I am so drawn to my mystical girl, but I lack the self-confidence to connect with her at the verbal and physical level.

I know intuitively that I am attached to Kathy for the emotional security. I cannot escape the strong force within me that pulls me towards my profound girl. I party the night away, and the next morning I enter Dunkin' Donuts.

I am sitting by the counter talking to a horseman, and the girl who puts me in a trance enters the door of Dunkin' Doughnuts; spontaneously I leap up and acknowledge her, shouting "Wow!" She gives me a smile, and I sit back down. It feels like I'm having an out-of-body experience, as my soul perceives a divinely-inspired prayer in her heart. She has such a powerful effect on me. I am hypnotized by her presence.

It is 5:30 a.m. and I have to get going, as I have a horse to work in a half an hour. Drew will be mad at me if I don't show up on time. Today is warm and sunny as I arrive at one of the barns, and the trainer puts me on a horse to work. We have to go six furlongs in a fast workout on the main track. The horsemen are standing by the rail, watching their horses. Fans are having breakfast trackside, and are captivated by the spell of Saratoga. I work my horse in a fast 1:09 for six furlongs, and the trainer is happy. I enter trainer Wayne Lukas's barn, and I don't see my enigmatic girl. I wonder whom she is working for?

Chapter 40

Serena

The sun is out and excitement is high in Saratoga this morning as I enter barn twelve. Chris and I have crossed paths and it has inflamed me with an electrifying force. I am so wowed by his presence, but at this moment in time I don't fully realize the depth of our connection.

What I do comprehend is how much I am in awe of him. I am saddling one of my horses, getting him ready for his daily workout. I turn my head and across the way, in the next stable, I see Chris. I'm just spellbound by his existence.

Back in this world, Eddie and I are hanging out. We are having fun going out on the town, and enjoying our time together. Maureen has been spending her time alone, and doesn't want to go out that much. Eddie and I respect her decision to be by herself.

After six weeks of being immersed in the allure of Saratoga, it's time to say goodbye. All the horses and horse people make their journey down the New York State Thruway back to Belmont Park. I have such an amazing experience, and now I am going back to Mommy Dearest. My delusion is still that I will be with Chris, and live happily ever after. My personality feels safe with Eddie, but my heart wants Chris.

My desire to be with Chris is just a fantasy. I have a severe handicap: after years of being the caretaker for my mother, I have a personality that appears able to take care of myself, but that is just a cover-up. My unfulfilled childhood need to have someone to depend on is controlling my life. With my need buried so deep within, there is no way I can ever live happily ever after with anyone, much less have a profound and intense connection.

How ironic that Eddie and I are just breaking up—we have an argument, and I unleash my fury upon him. I have such intense anger, and when I feel hurt, I lash out at whichever person I'm with. I can say some very cruel words. Eddie cannot forgive me, and now he's gone. I am alone again, but my daydream of being with Chris holds me together.

Chapter 41

Chris

I finish the 1988 Saratoga meet as one of the top five jockeys.

I had a great month and a half, but I was partying too hard. It caught up with me on August 24. I am riding a gelding (a colt who has been castrated) in the sixth race on the Saratoga turf course. My horse fractures his leg, and I pull him up. I jump off, but I let the reins go, and my horse runs off in pain to the wire.

The horse has to be put down, and I should have held on to the reins to keep him from running, but I was not thinking. I love horse racing, although some people think that it's cruel to run horses for this sport. Racehorses are bred to run—it takes all one's power to hold them back from breaking away from the rider. Thoroughbreds are my heart and soul, and I cannot imagine my life without them.

The enchantment of Saratoga lifts, as Kathy and I are driving on the thruway. Leaving upstate is like coming off a high, and making the transition from Saratoga is not easy. All the horses are back on Long Island, ready to run. I am riding in top form, but there is always a hint of danger, as you can be seriously injured or worse.

The danger comes on October 13, the fifth race on a nine-race card at Belmont Park. I am not riding in this race, but a horrific, tragic accident happens. My fellow jockey Mike Venezia is riding Mr. Walter K, a three-year-old gelding. His horse stumbles and breaks his right front leg, and Mike goes tumbling down. My girlfriend's brother, Robbie Davis, is riding Drums in the Night, who has no place to go but right over him, and the other jockeys hear a deathly scream. Robbie's horse is in full speed as his hooves thunder and pound into Mike's face.

The ambulance that follows all the races is at Mike's side in a heartbeat, but Mike Venezia is pronounced dead at the scene. Mike, who is forty-three years old, and was looking forward to retirement at the end of the year, is dead. All of us are stunned and shocked. Mike was a good guy. I feel for Robbie—it was not his fault. I can't imagine the guilt he must be feeling. The sport of horse racing is dangerous for the horse and horse people alike, but my passion for this game overrides any fear I might feel at the risks. I know most horse citizens feel the same way.

Chapter 42

Serena

I created unpleasant energy after my argument with Eddie, so I decide to look elsewhere for employment. I hear about a job opening in trainer Billy Badgett's barn. I'm on my way to Billy's right now. As I walk into his stable, I see Billy and ask, "I hear you are looking for a groom?"

Billy says, "Yes." Then he asks me, "When can you start?"

I say, "Tomorrow."

"Great, see you bright and early."

My father went to the races yesterday, and saw jockey Mike Venezia get killed. He feels really bad for the jockey and his family. A man at the races was complaining that they cancelled the racing. My father says to the guy, "A man just got killed; have some compassion."

After my break up with Eddie, I feel very alone. I haven't seen Chris in a couple of months. There has been a jockey strike at Aqueduct. Jockeys are the lowest paid athletes in this world, and probably in the most dangerous sport. A few days later, I hear that Chris and one of the scab riders, Billy Fox, got into a physical fight. It looks like Chris is letting out his anger, but still needs to learn how to do it in a healthy way.

In the meantime, jockey Billy Fox guides my filly Ingrid to victory in a twenty-two-thousand-dollar claiming race. The following week, I read in the newspaper that Chris is on his way to Japan to ride in the Fuji International Stakes. He is riding a horse named Salem Drive.

Right now I am traveling on a horse van to the Meadowlands Racetrack in New Jersey. My filly Ingrid is running in a race, scheduled to start at 11:30 p.m., and the dark-brown filly wins her race by two lengths. I was not too happy about going to New Jersey, but at least my horse won. I travel back by van, and arrive at Belmont Park at 3:00 a.m. Tomorrow I have the day off, and it feels good. Seven sunsets pass, and I read in the newspaper Chris has tested positive for drugs again.

Chapter 43

Chris

The New York jockeys want higher fees for their mounts, and I'm picketing with the other riders.

As time goes by, the regular riders are starting to ride again. One of the replacements, Billy Fox, is on a couple of horses on one particular day. Billy is accusing me of bringing him and his horse very wide on the turn. We exchange some heated words, and then next the thing I know Billy punches me in the left eye, and is fined five hundred dollars.

My anger is getting the best of me, but neither of us is held responsible for our riding abilities. Right now, I'm on a jet on my way to Japan; I'll be riding Salem Drive in the Fuji Stakes. I walk off the plane and am wowed by how friendly and polite I find the people here.

Horse racing is very big in Japan, and the racing facilities are top notch. I ride Salem Drive to victory in the Fuji Stakes, and I'm looking forward to coming back in two weeks to ride Salem Drive for the Japan Cup. On the plane going home, the movie *Big* is playing. I am crying at the end of the movie, because Tom Hanks's character has a problem growing up too fast, and wants to go back home.

Here I am a top jockey, and I just can't leave and go to rural South Carolina. Deep down, I know going back to my native land is what I need, so I can develop into an emotionally secure person. Understanding that is not going to happen, I decide to write a letter to God.

Dear God,

Since I was young, I've come a long way so very fast, and I'm not complaining about my success. But this is all (I have) and should I live the rest of my life the way it is now? I've pulled away from living and enjoying every minute of my life. When I am old, will I sit and think about the things that just flew by unnoticed, the things I just let pass me by, and the people that sometimes feel imaginary? God, you've given me so much talent, opportunity, money, friends, and people who really care for me. But do I really utilize all of these gifts to their best fulfillment? And am I truly happy?[xxix]

The aircraft has landed, and now I am in New York. Twenty-four hours after writing my letter to the Divine, I start using cocaine again. I go to work the next morning, and I am informed I am going to be drug tested again. Full of shame, I go to the bathroom, knowing I am going to test positive. I travel back to Japan two weeks later as I am worried they are going to take me off of my mount, but I am still able to ride Salem Drive in the Japan Cup; however, we unplaced in the race.

I don't want to go back to the Big Apple as I know I have tested positive. I am too ashamed at what might happen, and the press will have a field day over this. Reluctantly, I return, and Drew wants to see me right away. I drive to his house, and when I walk in, he sits me down and says to me, "We've been ruled off the racetrack."[xxx]

Chapter 44

Serena

An article in the *New York Daily News* says Chris Antley is suspended from riding. I automatically think I am going to become Chris's rescuer. I'm going to help him. The way my mind works is a habitual response from my upbringing. I am going to save Mommy Dearest, and in return I will get her love and approval.

What I don't fully comprehend is that Chris and I have a special bond. We are being kept apart for a good reason, as there is no way he or I can come together. *We have our own unhealthy problems, and the only people who can transform those issues are ourselves.* Chris is in rehab, and I have to find another trainer to work for. Billy Badgett is going to Florida with his horses, and is leaving at the end of December.

I find out a trainer a few stables down is looking for a groom. I walk into barn forty-nine and talk to Mr. Richie O'Connell. I ask Mr. O'Connell, "Do you need a groom?"

He says, "Yes."

I start work the next day. Mr. O'Connell has around twenty-five horses in his barn, and it feels to me like I might be staying here for a while. It's now winter in New York, and the barns are frigid, but the horses love the colder weather.

I hate the brisk temperature, and now I am looking forward to riding on the horse vans to Aqueduct Racetrack. I am saying that sardonically. If you remember last year, I had made up my mind to leave horses and find another avenue of work. Yet here I am working in the frost. It is so arctic on some mornings, my horse's water bucket clips are frozen together and I need a cigarette lighter to loosen the ice.

I am doing my daily routine with horses. I work out six days a week, mostly weight training. Three times a week, I jog on the treadmill, or do the Stairmaster. I will be in another bodybuilding competition sometime in March. Chris has been on my mind, and I wonder when I am going to see him again. Maybe this time we can merge, and I can rescue him. Do I think I need help at this time? The answer is no. I am fine, I tell myself, now that my mind is on Chris.

Fast-forward three days, and my father and I are in the den of my parents' house watching TV. When he says to me, "I think I was here before," he means in another lifetime. I didn't say anything, as I don't know what to make of the statement, but obviously my father is very intuitive, as he is aware of how he feels, knowing it is more of a subjective feeling, rather than an objective thought. What he says to me on this day will be stored in my unconscious, waiting for when the time is right to retrieve this memory.

Chapter 45

Chris

I am suspended from riding racehorses indefinitely.

Later, I explain it all to a reporter. "I didn't know what to do; I thought the world was over, I really did. I remained in my house for four to five days. I didn't want to go out in public because I didn't know if the papers had my story in it. I didn't know anything—I thought I couldn't ride anymore. I thought the world was at an end and started using cocaine for three days. I was going crazy. I used and used and my nose got so messed up, that I couldn't do it. I couldn't kill myself. It wouldn't kill me."[xxxi]

I find out if I enter rehab, I will have a chance to come back and ride. I take part in a twenty-eight-day program and I start to feel better after the first week. "They make you look at yourself. It was really scary how screwed up I was. They just don't make you look at the drug use and why you did it. They make you look at yourself and reality. They make you look at a lot of different things like friends and who you have—what's important in life. My whole life was working and people-pleasing. They had my whole life down. They could have written it down in one page."[xxxii]

The rehab facility wants us to call the most important people in our lives. The men and women start to call a partner, parent, or sibling. "I called my agent, Drew, which is when I started really realizing that in this world, that's who I have: Drew and the game. Other than that, I am getting closer to my family now, but Drew is like family: we work together in the morning and all through the day, and I can call on him when I have problems. I guess I realized the grind and the routine and making money wasn't everything."[xxxiii]

"It got to the point where it seemed like every day all I did was get up and come home and get up and go to the races and dream horses. Not that I didn't like it—I loved it, but I don't know, maybe inside I was wanting something else. I couldn't stop working, because I didn't know what to do when I had spare time; I had no clue."[xxxiv]

I complete my program, and now I'm changing my image. I sell my eighty-thousand-dollar white Mercedes-Benz with gold trim. Now I drive a 4x4 Blazer, and I have given up on having a nightlife. I am thinking about getting engaged to my girlfriend, and I hope the New York Racing Board will reinstate my license, so I can ride again. My wish is granted, and I am able to go back and ride at the end of January.

Chapter 46

Serena

On a beautiful morning in January of 1989, my father takes a ten-minute walk. Every day he ventures out to buy the *New York Daily News*. He sits down at the kitchen table, has breakfast, and makes some coffee. He opens the paper as he is eating and heads to the horse racing section. He looks to see if any horses look good to him so he can make a bet.

I come home from work and I see today's news is on the table. I open the newspaper and in the sports section it says that Chris Antley is coming back to ride. I haven't seen Chris in three months, but he has been on my mind every day. Chris is supposed to be coming back to ride this week…

I am grooming horses in barn forty-nine at Belmont Park. One day, I am saddling a dark bay filly named Berry Berry Nice. I walk out of the stall, and right before my eyes are two emerald, precious gems looking intently at me. I am floored that Chris catches me off guard; he is back not even one day and we are crossing paths again. Chris is in the barn to work Capades. Chris is being pulled toward me but has no idea what to do with what he knows. I think, "Why doesn't he want to talk to me?" I think that I am not worthy of his friendship, but I cannot escape the intense encounters we have. It is not like we are seeing each other across the barn. He comes right up to me, and looks deeply into my eyes.

A week later, Chris comes into the barn and works Wanderkin, a graded stakes gelding. Chris and Wanderkin are strutting around the barn. At this instant, Chris and I see each other and time stands still. My heart starts to beat a mile a minute. We fall into a deep trance as our souls emerge from our bodies. The shimmering caress of our love is piercing deep within me. My whole body is lustrously reverberating. It's as if we were making sweet, passionate love just by being in each other's presence.

The bond between us is intimately and profoundly deep. Little by little I am waking up from my sleep and realizing the pulsating beat of an astounding loved one. I feel Chris was born with the gift of sensing heaven in my eyes, and has the wisdom to understand the depth of me. My feelings and memories of these intense encounters are being stored in my subconscious. When the time is right, I will know what is being mysteriously conveyed to me.

Chapter 47

Chris

I complete my rehabilitation program.

In an interview, I later describe how I am feeling: "I feel like I died and started all over again. I call it my New Year's resolution because I got out of rehab the first of the year. It's totally different now. Just getting up in the morning every morning I feel good starting a new day."[xxxv]

The sun is inching its way up the horizon, and dawn is approaching. I take the fifteen-minute drive from Garden City to Elmont. I enter Belmont's main stable gate and make my way to barn forty-nine, Richie O'Connell's stable. Richie asks me if I can work Capades, whom the *New York Times* called one of the country's most accomplished three-year-old grass fillies.[xxxvi]

I march into the barn, and right away I am being pulled towards her: God, she is so beautiful. I am flowing with the force of the universe, and it feels awesome. It has been a couple of months since I last saw this girl who puts me in a trance. When I am in her presence, the magic she exudes embraces me in a spiritual rapture.

At the same time, I feel everyone hates me. Why would she like me? "I have paranoia about letting someone be close and share my feelings. I am hiding behind a wall, never showing that kind of identity. It is insecurity I guess."[xxxvii] I cannot escape the feeling that she just stepped out of a night vision, and somehow I am waking up out of that dream.

I am feeling the magic; a few days pass, and on February 8, I guide Lady Seaul to victory. I will continue to bring home at least one winner a day for the next couple of months. It feels good staying sober and winning races. Life is fabulous right now!

Chapter 48

Serena

It is the first half of the year of 1989. I am numb to my anger, hurt, and fear, and I am living in denial of my emotions. Chris is ahead of me at this moment in time. He had some psychotherapy in rehab. I, on the other hand, do not have any conscious clue about my issues. Chris is very intuitive, and can sense our spiritual connection. Chris is waking me up so that I can become more knowledgeable about our eternal gift.

I feel there is one avenue where I am ahead of Chris: I am home creating a strong foundation. Chris does not have the luxury to go back to his roots and create an emotionally hardy sense of self. He can go home—there is always a choice—but he would risk losing his career as a top jockey.

One day, I have a horse in a race, and Chris Antley is scheduled to ride. I'm so excited and happy! He is on my horse! He is on my horse! I have a plan: I am going to say something to him while he is on my horse.

I am parading my filly in the paddock area of Aqueduct Racetrack. Chris gets a leg up and I ask him, "How are you doing?" He doesn't respond to me, and I am devastated. I feel so low, because in my mind I think I am not worthy enough.

My filly runs a poor race, and now my horse and I are in this disgusting van going back to Belmont Park, and we stop for a red light. I am sitting on a water bucket next to my horse's stall. As the truck is stopped at the light, I see Chris Antley in his car with his girlfriend, Kathy. I am feeling like a servant, feeling worthless.

The next morning, Chris is in my barn, but now I feel rejected and don't want to acknowledge him, but he comes up to me, and we are mesmerized by each other again. Chris knows we are linked, but his personality is in utter confusion. I am totally frustrated. He rejected me, but now he seems to want to make it up by nonverbally saying, don’t take that as a dismissal, for my soul loves your inner essence.

Chapter 49

Chris

The May flowers are blooming, and I end my sixty-four-day winning streak.

I don't get a winner for the first time in a long time, but that is OK. I set what could be a permanent record. I am nicknamed Joe DiMaggio, after the Yankee who had a fifty-six-game hitting trend. The press built it up a little; anytime you are pushing, hoping to keep a streak going, there is extra pressure.[xxxviii]

Drew feels this feat will never be bettered. To show my appreciation, I buy dozens of donuts from Dunkin' Donuts and give them to various barns. The grooms, the hot walkers, the exercise people—they're the people who brought the horse to the winner's circle. They don't get the glory that I do.[xxxix] I was suspended for rough riding back in April, and will take those days in June. As the summer approaches, I head to Atlantic City for my holiday. I have free time, and I start to use cocaine again, which affects every part of my life.

I head to Saratoga, and I'm still enmeshed with cocaine. At the end of the meet, I am thrown after a race and tear ligaments in my knee, so I have to be out for a few days. I have a lot of fear within when I have downtime, so I use drugs to numb me.

My engagement to Kathy has just ended, and now I'm an emotional wreck. I am attached to Kathy, and the loss of this emotional resource has left me fearful. My personality is being reduced to particles after the breakup, and has destroyed the cohesion of my fragile ego.

If anything can go wrong it will, and now I have to surrender my jockey's license. The New York Racing Association wants me to take another drug test. I know I will not pass, so I just surrender the license.

Drew says that I am a natural. I do brilliant things on a horse, and can ride effortlessly.[xl] But he cannot take my dysfunction any longer. He later explains how he felt to a journalist: “I had no alternative than to do what I did. I am physically sick about this whole thing. I just hope that the future treats Chris kindly.”[xli] Drew fears for my life, and people say, “He is an enabler.”[xlii]

Drew and I part ways, but I feel bad and will miss him terribly. I put myself back into rehab, and if I successfully complete the program again, I might have another chance to get my license back. I have created material wealth, but my emotional life is impoverished. I feel like a victim, and my emotional sense of my own value is nil. I need to go home and find out what my issues are. For now, I am back at rehab; I’m not sure if this will give me the trust or the internal sense of security I need, but I have to go to rehab if I ever want to ride again.

Chapter 50

Serena

Every week that passes in this last year of the 1980s, Chris crosses paths with me. I am still numbing myself with my addictions—from working out, to having sex at different times with a couple of men. My heart and soul want to hook up with Chris.

From beginning to end, I am frustrated. Here I am inches away from a gorgeous man, who comes up to me and takes a long mesmerizing look, only to walk away and say nothing. My personality is emotionally attached to him, and I am still daydreaming that one day we are going to get together. I am blind in this moment to his dysfunctional issues, and ignorant of my own problems.

One day I am working out at Metrofit, a gym on Long Island. I hear Drew is a member, so I introduce myself to Drew's personal trainer and ask him, "Do you train Drew Mollica?"

The trainer says, "Yes." Then I ask him about Chris. He says, "One day, Drew is going to find him dead in a hotel room."

His true if negative statement goes right over my head. I am going to help Chris, as I am ready to be his savior. How absolutely absurd my mind is reasoning at this time. I have had this mindset since day one of my life: I am going to make Mommy Dearest happy, then I will get her love in return.

This is the same dysfunctional thinking I have with Chris: I am going to help him, and then I will get his love. But our bond, which I don't fully understand at this point, is divinely inspired. There is no way that a blessed connection could ever, ever withstand such unhealthy ways. When I read that Chris Antley has been ruled off from riding indefinitely, my personality falls to pieces. I feel as if I am losing my emotional resource, even if it is only in my mind. I never had emotional security as a child. I grew up mentally and emotionally impoverished.

I never have the luxury of feeling secure, emotionally or materially. I was not granted such richness, and I never act wisely when it comes to money or relationships. Money is not abundant in my family of origin.

My older sister Mary Lou doesn't have the same issues as I do. My mother welcomed Mary Lou into her life, so whatever Mary Lou wants, she receives. Fran, my middle sister, acquired less than Mary Lou, but still obtains what she desires. Since I was not wanted from my conception, I am given very little. Deep down in my subconscious, I always have the feeling that danger is ahead, and I never know if I am going to survive.

Chapter 51

Chris

I get my jockey license reinstated in March of 1990.

Having been in rehab for a couple of months, I feel fantastic, and have a whole new outlook on life. I now have a new agent, and we seem to be working great together. I am a little apprehensive about going back to the racetrack since I'm worried how the fans are going to react. To my surprise, everyone is very supportive. I am in the saddle again, and I win three races on the first day.

I stroll into barn forty-nine a few days later and see my heart-pounding, brown-eyed girl. After all this time, I am still drawn to her—it's as if I never left. A force within me draws me to her, like bees are drawn to honey. I am not going out with Kathy anymore, and I sure would love to go out with her. But my insecurities are saying, "I am not worth loving or knowing," so I just keep gazing intently into her eyes, hoping to connect verbally with her, but knowing I can't.

I'm under the spell of Saratoga, and I accomplish an unbelievable feat. I win the Saratoga riding title, and it feels awesome. Saratoga is where the best horses, trainers, and jockeys compete. My dear friend, jockey Angel Cordero Jr., is king of Saratoga, winning the title eleven times in a row, so to be here with him and winning the title is an honor.

Two months go by, and I'm riding a horse named Mr. Nickerson in the one-million-dollar Breeder's Cup Sprint at Belmont Park. The Breeders Cup was created a few years before, honoring a fun-filled day of the richest horse races in America. During the race, my horse either has a heart attack, or ruptures an artery, and he goes down. I am thrown to the ground. Mr. Nickerson has to be euthanized back at the barn.

Two races later is the one-million-dollar Breeders' Cup Distaff. Champion filly Go for Wand, with Randy Romero up, and trained by Billy Badgett, and an Argentine mare Bayakoa with Laffit Pincay Jr. in the irons, are going stride for stride. Go for Wand has a head in front and is winning with a sixteenth of a mile to go, when Go for Wand shatters her right foreleg. This is the worst, most shocking breakdown in Breeders' Cup history, and Go for Wand has to be euthanized right on the track. Her foreleg is beyond repair.

Racehorses run their hearts out, and are courageous athletes. Unfortunately, like in any sport, there is always the risk of injury. There isn't a dry eye on this race day. I wake up in the hospital with a broken collarbone, and am out of commission for a couple of months. I start to use drugs again, but for a while I feel able to keep it under control.

Chapter 52

Serena

The gym is calling me to train six days a week, since I have entered another bodybuilding contest. I work out intensely with heavy weights. Three times a week my heart beats faster and faster on the Stairmaster. My strict diet of bland foods plus fruits and vegetables is making me irritable. I drop to eight percent body fat, down from my normal fifteen percent.

All my hard work pays off, and I win the Ms. Mets bodybuilding contest. Not only do I come in first in my weight class, but I triumph as the overall winner. The show is being aired on the Madison Square Garden network channel. My victory helps me appear in a couple of bodybuilding magazines, showing off my physique. I am finally getting some admiration, but does it help my self-esteem? The answer is "No." My family or friends are not there to see me win. The only people who support me are the people from the gym. I feel with support comes strength, but I only have power in my muscles, not in myself.

My sister Fran is getting married in a month and a half—on my birthday. She told me last year that she picked April first for her wedding date, and I went ballistic. I always felt having my birthday on April Fool's Day was special. Now, she is intruding on my parade.

It is pure chaos in my house the day I find out she is getting married in April. I am telling Fran how I feel in an angry voice. She starts yelling at me, and then Mommy Dearest starts hollering. Mommy Dearest is in the bathroom screaming, and I am trying to say how I feel, but Mommy Dearest does not care. All she says, as she is screeching and crying, is, "Leave me alone, you bitch."

The whole family including myself, mother, father and Fran are going to Mary Lou's house that day. My mother says to my father and sister, "Don't tell anyone what happened." I am the bad daughter, as I caused this misfortune. I spend the day in my niece's room, crying my eyes out. The only person at the end of the day who comes to see me is my brother in-law, Steve.

Needless to say, Fran ties the knot on April Fool's Day, 1990. My family half-heartedly wishes me a happy birthday. I am numb, and don't realize it; I'm also not fully aware that I'm in a state of depression, but that is all going to change very soon.

It is June 30, 1990, and I wake up early, and head off to work. I see Chris and we are intrigued by each other as usual. He is to breeze Wanderkin, which he does. An hour later, I ask Wanderkin's groom, "Who is going to ride him?"

The man says, "Chris Antley." Then he adds, "Chris likes you."

That is all I need to hear. My mind is elated. I go home, work out, and then start driving to my sister's, since I have committed myself to babysit my niece and nephew for the night.

It is a beautiful sunny day in New York, and the temperature is around eighty degrees. It's 7:00 p.m., and by an act of fate I am driving in the middle lane on Sunrise Highway in Merrick. The car behind me wants to go faster. The driver goes into the right lane and is accelerating when the car in front of him makes a right turn. I hear a very loud noise!

The driver immediately slows down, but he doesn't have enough time to stop, so he decides to come into my lane. He hits the passenger side of my car, and the impact causes the two passenger wheels to come off my car, so I never regain control of my vehicle. I go flying across the right-hand lane onto the curb of the sidewalk, knocking over a stop sign along the way. From that point on, I am unconscious, and my car flips over several times.

My vehicle is completely crushed, except for where I was. Luckily, I regain consciousness right after the impact. I wake up inside my car, right side up, while my car is upside down. The first thought that comes into my mind is, *the car is going to blow up—get out of the car*. I am not wearing my seatbelt, and I crawl through my crushed window. I am in a state of shock as I'm viewing my car, and the damage it has suffered. I think, *my father is going to kill me*.

I see the driver of the other car, and I yell to him, "Why were you going so fast?" People start to come out of the woodwork as they pull me away, and sit me down on the sidewalk. The paramedics come, and bring me into the ambulance. A lady asks if she can phone someone for me, so I ask her to phone my sister Mary Lou to tell her what has happened.

Mary Lou comes to the site of the accident, and as soon as I see her all I want is a hug. I am emotional: after all, I just escaped death. When I put my arms around her, she pushes me away, and says to me, "I thought you were tougher than that." I am stunned, and don't know what to say.

The paramedics say, "You should have been dead on arrival." A nurse in the hospital says, "Someone up there must like you." The doctors say, "You should have seven surgeons over you." I walk into the emergency room without a scratch on me.

Chapter 53

Serena

I am in the emergency room of the hospital after my car accident. I am lying in bed, and the nurses are doing blood tests on me. The doctor wants to know if I was drinking alcohol. Can you believe it? I am the victim, and they want to know if I am under the influence. I was not drinking or doing drugs. I was going to babysit.

Mary Lou follows me to the hospital, and is complaining to the nurses. She wants to know when I am going to be released. One of the nurses approaches me, and says, "You were lucky once today. You need to rest. You don't need to babysit those brats." I don't say anything, but deep down I understand what she is telling me.

The nurse sees right through my sister. I am being treated like a servant and I need to take care of myself. A couple of minutes later my parents come to see me. They are concerned about my well-being, and want to know what happened. They just can't believe something like this could happen. I am released within a couple of hours, but that whole night I can't sleep as I am replaying the whole scenario.

I do not go to work the next day, as I just need the rest. My body aches from the traumatic impact. Within the next couple of weeks, my lower back starts to hurt. Now I'm going to the chiropractor, and he tells me I have rights. I should seek a lawyer. He gives me the name of an attorney, and my father and I go to see him. He takes my case, and the lawyer wants me to be out of work for six months. I am not so thrilled at this idea, as I didn't know what I will do with myself if I am not working. Then it occurs to me I will not see Chris again, but I decide to take the time off. Now I have a lot of spare time on my hands.

People say to me how lucky I am to be alive, but I do not feel grateful. I should have been dead, and I want to know why I am not. Having so much free time makes me realize how unhappy I really am.

After two weeks, I seek out some form of work. I am at my gym and ask a girl who works there, "Where can I pick up clients to train?" She leads me to a personal training center in Hewlett. One day I go and talk with the owner, who is a couple of years older than I am. I don't feel like I care whether I get the job or not. He says that I will be on the books. I then get up, and start to leave. Then, in happy shock, I say, "I can't be."

He says, "We can work something out."

I stay and I become a personal fitness trainer. In my mind, being at the gym is only temporary, as I will go back to working with horses.

A couple of months later, after Chris wins the Saratoga riding title, I visit barn forty-nine at Belmont Park. I see they need help, so I just start to walk a horse. I miss being around these awesome creatures. Now I have the best of both worlds: I'm at Belmont Park on the weekends, and during the week, I work at the personal training gym. I have not seen Chris in a couple of months, but he has never left my mind, and I am always looking in the newspaper to see how many races he has won.

I am still questioning why I am alive when I should have been dead. I am visiting Mary Lou one day, and as we are talking, I say, "I am worried about Daddy." He has been getting sicker by the month. He has Chronic Obstructive Pulmonary Disease—emphysema—and I am afraid he is going to die. Then I ask my sister, "Why am I still alive?"

She says something very profound: "Don't you want to find out why you didn't die?"

I don't say anything, but I think it made sense. Yet at the time, I can't fully appreciate the statement. I am now in such a deep state of depression, I start to cry, and she leaves the room, leaving me feeling empty and lost.

Chapter 54

Chris

I have recovered from my injury.

I am back in the saddle again. Here I am, twenty-five years old, and I have yet to win a Kentucky Derby. It is early in the year of 1991. My agent and I are on the lookout for some Derby prospects. I have two likely starters for the Derby. One is a filly, Meadow Star, who is nine for nine. The other is a colt who won the Florida Derby, named Strike the Gold.

Strike the Gold's trainer Nick Zito, a dark-haired, deep-voiced, native New Yorker—and a friend—needs a rider for the Bluegrass Stakes. Nick praises me, and describes me to others thus: "To me, Chris was always a special person and an unbelievable talent. The kid never ceased to amaze me. It was just something that was God-given."[xliii]

I fly to Kentucky to ride Nick's colt. It is a rainy day in Keeneland, and the track is labeled good. Strike the Gold and I are wearing sky-blue and pink for the colors of the owners. We are in the starting gate and—boom!—we are off on the backside, trailing by six lengths. On the top of the stretch I ask my colt to move, and we win the Bluegrass Stakes easily by three lengths. Days later I am in the barn area of Belmont and I discover Meadow Star is out of the Kentucky Derby, so I will be riding Strike the Gold.

It is May 4, 1991, and I am in the paddock for the 117th running of the Kentucky Derby. A crowd of 135,554 has gathered at the famed twin spires of Churchill Downs. The weather is cloudy, and the track is labeled fast.

Sixteen colts have entered the prestigious race, and I am third choice behind Hansel and Fly So Free. Nick Zito says this about Strike the Gold, "[H]e's a horse of destiny. His mother died when he was four months old. His father, Alydar, died last Nov. 15 on the same day Strike the Gold won his first race. You had to believe he was destined for great things."[xliv] Alydar was the archrival to the last Triple Crown winner, Affirmed. In 1978 Alydar ran second to Affirmed in each of the Triple Crown races.

Riders are up, and we are going to the post parade. "My Old Kentucky Home" is playing and tears are rolling down my face: I can feel I am going to win today. We are in the starting gate and we are off; my horse breaks sharply.

We are twelfth at the half-mile pole running easy, and my dear friend Angel Cordero is on Quintana outside of me. After the race, I tell the newscaster what happens then. "Angel looks over, and he says, 'How much horse you got, Poppy?' And I said 'Well, I'm sitting pretty good right now…I got a good bit of horse.'"[xlv]

At the three-quarter pole, I am nudging my colt to pick up the pace, and we are seventh. At the top of the stretch, we are on the far outside. Down the stretch we come, and I am in the middle of the racetrack. My horse just switches leads, and I am whipping him from left to right, with a sixteenth of a mile to go. We do it! We pass the wire first! I raise my whip in the air…Strike the Gold and I have just won the Kentucky Derby!

Two weeks pass, and the elation I feel at the Derby is overshadowed by today's events. It is May 18, and Strike the Gold and I are elegantly walking in the post parade, while "Maryland, My Maryland" is performed by the military band. It is a chilly, cloudy day here just outside Baltimore, with 87,245 people in attendance for the race.

It is now post time for the 116th running of the Preakness Stakes. We are in the gate, and we're off. I am lying eighth in a field of eight. "Being down on the inside, maybe he didn't like that. When we got to running, it got a little tighter. He never got his mind on running."[xlvi] We finished sixth in a field of eight, and Hansel with Jerry Bailey up wins the Preakness by seven lengths. Yet, I feel confident that Strike the Gold will come back in three weeks for the Belmont Stakes.

It is a clear, warm day in New York for the 123rd running of the Belmont. A crowd of 51,766 has gathered at Belmont Park to watch this highly esteemed race. I am in the paddock, and the call for riders up is announced.

I am on Strike the Gold, and we are proceeding to the track for the post parade. I can faintly hear Frank Sinatra's song, "New

York, New York," sung in the background. It is now post time, and we are at the starting gate.

They're off! My horse breaks well, and we are trailing the eleven-horse field down the backside. Around the far turn, I am passing horses left and right. At the top of the stretch, I am in good striking distance. Down the stretch we come, and we are flying on the outside. Hansel is in front, and I am going to catch him. We are just at the wire and—oh no!—Hansel wins the Belmont Stakes by a head. When you lose by a head, you have a million questions. I kept pleading with him, come on Strike, hurry up and kick in. I just wish it was a mile and a half and four jumps.[xlvii] If it had been, I would have crossed the wire first.

Chapter 55

Serena

I am opening up my heart to my sister Mary Lou, but she cannot deal with feelings. This is my dysfunctional family. I am living in a narcissistic environment where the family members are disconnected from each other emotionally, so there is no real sense of closeness or trust. My father and I trust and love with all our heart, but the unhealthy interaction between my mother and sisters dominates.

At this moment in time, I am starting on a journey and I am taking the road less traveled. My car accident is a wakeup call, telling me it's time to start understanding myself. Without comprehending my fears and limitations, there is no way I can lead a fulfilling life. I don't fully understand all the trauma and drama of my childhood, but now I am rousing from my sleep, and starting my trip down the freeway.

I venture on the path by taking a leap. I see an ad in a magazine: *Come to the Berkshire Mountains of Connecticut on a fitness weekend.* It sounds exciting, so I book the trip and I am going in a month. I am really nervous as I am venturing outside my safety zone. I am having a lot of anxiety and I want to cancel, but I decide to do it. My father drives me to Manhattan, and I catch a bus to Connecticut.

I am so jittery, feeling fearful as I wonder whom I am going to talk to. Everyone on the bus is going to Club Getaway, and I instantly make friends. Needless to say, I have the time of my life at Club Getaway. I am meeting people, and I'm enjoying the fitness classes. I even rappel down a mountain. The hours go by too fast, and by the time I turn around the weekend is over.

My father, mother, and Fran pick me up in the city, and I tell them what a great time I had. My mother jumps in and says, "This is it. No more going away." I had the best time, and I am not going to listen to her. I go home and continue working with people at the gym, but I really don't know what to do: should I go back and work with horses full time, or stay put? I haven't seen Chris in months, but he has been on my mind. I decide I will continue at the personal training center, and on the weekends visit the exquisite animals.

Chapter 56

Serena

As I am working at the personal training gym, I meet two very important people. One of my clients is a wealthy man named Joe, who is interested in owning racehorses. I introduce Joe to my weekend boss Mr. Richie O'Connell. Mr. O'Connell leads him in the right direction, and Joe buys his first racehorse.

I am very happy knowing that I can bring new people into the dying sport of horse racing. Joe is on his way to having some success owning thoroughbreds. I am also training a woman Lorrelle, who is a psychotherapist at a local college. When we are talking one day, I am telling her about my life, and she says I should go to the school and seek a therapist. Then Lorrelle says something very profound: *Psychotherapy is like making a study of yourself.* Her statement hit home: since my car accident, I have been waking up thinking that something is wrong with me, and I really want to find an answer. I want to know why I did not die in my car accident.

I drive to Adelphi and seek assistance. The therapist I will be seeing is an intern, and I will be with her for a year and a half. The school has a sliding scale method of payment, so I can afford to go. We set up a schedule where I will be in therapy three times a week. My first visit is very interesting; I sit on a chair, and the therapist doesn't say anything. She waits for me to start chatting, so I ask her, "What shall we talk about?" I don't have any clue what to discuss, so I just start making comments about the day, nothing very deep.

As time progresses, I start communicating about my father and his sickness. I discuss how my mother is very critical and unsupportive, and how my sisters just follow her lead. Since discovering my newfound bravery while traveling alone, I book a cruise to the Bahamas. My therapist thinks this is a little spontaneous. As I will be leaving in fourteen days, I am looking forward to it.

Two days before I say bon voyage, I am watching the Kentucky Derby. I see Chris win the Derby on Strike the Gold. My personality is detaching from Chris, but deep down he is right there in my subconscious mind.

As Monday morning arrives I fly to Miami, Florida and I board a ship named the *Fantasy*. The boat docks in the Bahamas, with stops in Nassau and Freeport. My travel agent hooks me up with a couple of other singles, and we have a great time. I meet a guy named Tim who looks like Chris, and we are having fun. On the island of Nassau, my new friend Tim and I are soaking up the sun's rays. That night, as the first quarter moon is shining, I dance the night away with my roommate Lisa in the Cat's Lounge.

I drink so much tequila the next night, I am sick in my sleep. My room attendant starts cleaning me up while I am in a comatose state. I wake up the next morning not realizing how sick I am, and say "Someone please stop the ship!" as the boat is rocking back and forth. I look at the time and observe, *"It's horse racing time!"* I noticed yesterday that on today's schedule it said: *Come and cheer your favorite horses as they race down the track!* I want to go, so I enter the Universe Lounge, but I am not feeling great. I don't participate as I'm running to the bathroom every five minutes.

The rest of the day I recover from my hangover. At night, I watch the sunset at 7:45 p.m. I have a late dinner, and a mellow evening with my new friends. I have only two more days on my cruise, so I am appreciating the open sea. It is exhilarating as I feel my first taste of traveling the world in a very unique way. It's now time to disembark and head to the airport. Tim and Lisa are on a different flight as they live in Arizona and Michigan. Hopefully, we will stay in touch.

The plane has landed, and I am home. I tell my therapist the next day I had a wonderful time. I am telling her I didn't worry, I made friends, I was happy. I was so delighted being away, I didn't want to come back. For that moment in time, I was very content. A month later my therapist and I discuss how people think that I am confident, tough, and snobby. I say that I am shy, and I feel like a monster. I assume people think bad things about me, so I act distant or mean so they don't reject me first. I tell her that my mother makes me feel unlovable, so I have deep anger within and I can lash out at any time. My mother always puts me down, and says to me, "You hang out with nuts. Get lost."

A couple of weeks go by and Joe has a horse in a race. Chris Antley will be riding Joe's horse! It is July 17, and I am in the paddock at Belmont Park on this beautiful, hot, sunny day with Joe and Mr. O'Connell. They Are All Crazy is being saddled for his race, then Chris Antley gets a leg up and proceeds to the track for the post parade. Chris and I are not close enough to make our awe-inspiring connection with each other, but we can sense the magic between us. They Are All Crazy wins the eighteen-thousand-dollar claiming race!

Chapter 57

Chris

I have just finished the Triple Crown races with Strike the Gold.

The run for the Triple Crown is nerve racking, but electrifying at the same time. It's now a month and a half later, and I am riding at Belmont Park. It is a hazy, hot, and humid day in New York, and I'm in the paddock for an eighteen-thousand-dollar claiming race. I get a leg up on the horse and I see her, the girl who puts me in a trance, whom I have not seen in months. I wonder where she has been.

You know I don't have the confidence to ask her. It's as if I saw her yesterday. She is so bewitching to me. I win the race by two lengths, and we are in the winner's circle together, and our picture is taken. The races are moving to Saratoga next week. I am looking forward to getting up there, as a change of scenery is nice.

It's Friday July 26, the first weekend of the Saratoga meet. It's early in the evening, and I look up at the night sky as the bright, full moon is dazzling. I am wearing khakis with a nice shirt, the west wind is blowing my styled hair, and I skip onto Caroline Street. I decide to go to Gaffney's, a bistro and bar. I enter the restaurant and proceed to the outside bar, passing by some tables, and oh my God, I see her...

A strong force within me is pulling me towards her. She is sitting at a table with two men, but I don't care. A dynamic momentum is propelling me. I approach, and I am standing two inches away from her, and I don't know what to do. You know how you sometimes stare so hard, trying to make something happen?[xlviii] I just stand there looking intently at her big, brown eyes, waiting for her to say something.

I kept staring and staring,[xlix] but she doesn't say anything. In the end, I just walk away from the table and go down the stairs to the bar. An hour goes by and I'm at the bar having a drink, when my heart-pounding girl comes down the stairs, and we are now side by side. My soul is saying, "I love you," but my personality doesn't have the courage to say that to her. I leave alone, about an hour and a half later.

Two days pass and on July 28, I ride Strike the Gold to a third-place finish in the Jim Dandy Stakes. Days later, the owners of Strike the Gold take me off of him. They thought I didn't give him a good enough ride. They put Angel Cordero Jr. on him for the midsummer Derby. Strike the Gold comes in fourth behind Corporate Report, Hansel, and Fly So Free in the Travers Stakes.

I am lonely. Kathy and I are not together, and there is no way I can be with the girl who puts me in a trance. By the universal cosmic flow, my agent and I are at a shopping center in Saratoga when I see her. My royal girl is strutting towards us and my agent says, "You should ask her out." I want to so badly, but I do not have the power to make a wise choice.

Chapter 58

Serena

I am on my way to Saratoga with my dog Romeo, and arrive a few days early to set up the barn for Mr. O'Connell. A friend of mine and two other people are renting a house on the lake. I am looking forward to taking Romeo for long walks by the water.

I am driving on an open highway in Saratoga, and for one second I am at peace. For one split moment in time I am detached from Chris and at one with my mind and the universe. I experience a sense of oneness with all of life. I glimpse what it is like to have a serene mind. It does not last for very long.

The next day, my friend Derek is driving here from Long Island. We are going to be hanging out with another male friend of mine, and decide to go to Gaffney's for dinner. It is a balmy night so we decide to eat outside, and the waitress seats us at a table in the corner of the restaurant.

Three horses in full gallop with their jockeys riding their mounts to the wire are painted on the brick wall behind me. Perhaps they are inspired by the European nineteen-century-realist painter Edgar Degas's depiction of French horse races. I am dressed in a black mini-skirt and an off-the-shoulder white top and heels—I look hot! We order drinks, and the next thing I know I see Chris. He is approaching me and comes right up to my face and just stands there.

The hypnotic trance I am in is intoxicating. Our souls are revering each other as our exalted bond pulses through my body and out to the universe. Our souls are whispering, "Hey it's me, don't you see?" Our personalities are very confused. I am waiting for him to say something, but he does not say anything. My friends think the encounter is a little strange.

An hour passes as Chris and I are at the bar area, standing side by side, not saying a word. Our souls are screaming, "I love you." I see Chris about a week after this magical experience, at an outside shopping mall in Saratoga. Chris is walking with his agent, and we pass each other. I hear his agent say to him, "You should ask her out." Nothing comes of the incident, and I get in my car and leave.

I have an awesome time for the rest of the month. I am working during the day, and going out at night, enjoying myself. One day I take a thirty-minute drive on the Northway, entering the Lake George area. I park my car on a residential street, and Romeo and I cross a pedestrian bridge and hike Mt. Prospect. It is amazing to see my dog instinctually know where to step, and where not to.

A couple of days later I meet my friend Tony for drinks on his boat. We are cruising on Saratoga Lake, and I start to tell him about my face-to-face encounters with Chris. He says, "Maybe he doesn't want to be seen with just a hot walker." I don't say anything to Tony but the shame cuts through me like a knife. Tony is telling me how I feel about myself: I'm not worthy of being with Chris. A similar situation occurs when one of my friends witnesses Chris and me staring at each other—my friend asks me if I like Chris, and of course I say no, because I don't want him to tell me that I am not worthy.

The Saratoga meet is coming to a close, and on the last night I see Chris's car on Broadway. I immediately call a friend to see if she wants to go out, but she doesn't. I still want to see if Chris and I are ever going to hook up. The next day, I have to leave Saratoga, and I am out of my wits crying, as I don't want to go back home. I have to go back, but before I leave, an interesting event happens.

The idea that Chris and I are going to get together just falls asleep in my mind. The time is right for me to detach from the idea that Chris and I will ever be with each other. I don't feel valuable enough to be with him. I decide he is just an intense attraction that will never come to be.

Chapter 59

Chris

The end of the Saratoga meet is here, and I did OK in the standings but not great.

The last night in upstate New York, I go drinking at one of the restaurants in town; the next day I'm up early, and I head towards Long Island. I do fine for the rest of 1991: I manage to win 215 races for the year, and my total earnings are eight million and change.

Unfortunately, I think I have only one or two more good years within me. I've lost my drive, and don't know if I can get it back. I'm just going through the motions of life. I don't have any self-value, and it's a struggle just to exist. Of course, I am still using drugs and alcohol. I am trying to keep it under control, but for how long I have no idea. I am starting to find that keeping my riding weight at 115 pounds is getting really hard, as I love to eat, and can't eat what I want.

The last time I saw my heart-pounding girl was in Saratoga, and I don't know when I'll see her again. It is just as well, since I can't see myself getting together with her. She probably doesn't even like me.

Now I find out I've grown one and a half inches, a nightmare coming true. I am twenty-six years old, how can this be? It is correct—no wonder it's been getting harder for me to keep my weight. I feel like I'm sinking into a hole and don't know how to get out. I feel worthless as people talk about me and my addictions. I am very isolated, and that lonely feeling puts me in a deep depression, and I turn my anger inward as my life passes me by.

Chapter 60

Serena

Chris falls asleep in my mind as I let go of the idea we will ever be together. My addiction to sex is still controlling my life. I meet a guy in Saratoga who lives on Long Island. We have a one-night stand, but he wants more and so do I. He keeps calling my parents' house. These are the days before cell phones became popular. My mother is asking, "Who is this man?" She says to me, "You are up to something."

I am twenty-five years old and Mommy Dearest is making me feel as if I am doing something wrong, just by wanting to date. I don't say anything to her, but I know this is wrong. This is why I have to hide my sexual liaisons. I attract sexual attention and praise, but deep down I want to be loved for myself.

After a while the man stops calling, but then I secretly hook up with another guy. I resume therapy, and tell my therapist what a great time I had in Saratoga and how I didn't want to come back. Therapy is the best solution for me, since I desperately need to get out my frustrations about my mother's critical voice and my father's illness.

I am severely depressed, and I don't know how to overcome my depression. I am not taking antidepressants, but I feel that not taking them is a good decision for me. I feel antidepressants will just mask my issues, and for me, not being dependent on them is a wise choice. I am happy in certain situations, but when I come down from that high, I am lost and empty. I don't make enough money at this time to move out of my parents' house, but I don't think I'm ready yet anyway; the guilt would kill me, knowing I left my father while he was so ill.

I spend the rest of the year sneaking out for a night here or there to be with the man I'm seeing. We are just having sex, but I become emotionally attached to him. He doesn't really want anything to do with me, and I become distraught. I am so lonely, knowing no one loves me, that I become suicidal. I continue falling farther down until I hit rock bottom, and don't know how to escape the darkness.

I am not good enough; I hate myself; I just want to die and end the pain. My sisters are good daughters, while I am such a bad person. I must be awful—my mother and sisters say I am. All I want is to be accepted by them. I want them to support me, but I don't have that luxury.

I am fearful my father is going to die and leave me all alone. Since my car accident, I have been borrowing my father's car, so when I see a vehicle I like, I ask my father if he will co-sign the loan for me. My mother goes berserk: she doesn't want my father to help me. She says I don't deserve it. She is not giving me the car. I have to work to pay for it.

Eventually, my father co-signs the loan. It is here I say everything I feel I need to say to him before he dies. I say, "Daddy, I love you, and I don't know what I will do without you."

He says, "I love you too. Maybe if I get this operation, I will live another couple of years."

Chapter 61

Chris

The scale in the year 1992 is not my best friend.

My growth spurt is making it getting harder and harder for me to make my riding weight. Most people think that since jockeys are so small, we are naturally light. This is a misconception: our bodies are as well-defined, as our muscles are pumped. Jockeys are the only people who need to step on a scale every day.

I put two fingers down my throat to make myself flip (vomit). The trauma that I cause makes my esophagus upchuck the food I just ate. After my self-inflicted torture, I immediately jump in the steam room and sweat off (I hope) five pounds. The moist heat is unbearable: I can't breathe, but I will not be able to ride today if I leave. I need to tough it out. I feel like burning wax, dripping and dripping as the candle melts.

I find it intolerable waking up every day having to reduce, and I ingest water pills and laxatives. A very common difficulty jockeys live with is the requirement to stay light enough to get mounts. Then once you have the call on the horse, you have to be strong enough at the low weight to ride a twelve-hundred-pound animal. I just hope in the future of this sport, people will have compassion for us, and up the weight requirements.

In the past, doing cocaine helped with my body mass, but now even that is not working and it is a taking a toll on my body. I should be about 130 pounds on my five-foot, three-inch frame. To ride, I have to be no more than 115 pounds.

I eat very little, and what I do eat I have to vomit. I am getting more frustrated by the minute and I don't have the spark of life I once had. I am not breaking records anymore. I am lonely, and I am not running into the girl who puts me in a trance.

I am very frustrated, and I let my anger out on the racetrack. I am suspended four times this year for aggressive riding. Then on a cold, dreary, November day at Aqueduct I am riding a two-year-old gelding in the sixth race. I am involved in a spill as my horse, Koluctoo Jimmy Al, clips heels with another horse. My horse falls, then gets up and runs until he is caught. I suffer four fractured ribs.[l]

I am going deeper into depression. I am five to seven pounds over in the morning. I describe the struggle to a *New York Times* reporter: "It means stepping into the day is difficult. You wake up worrying how light you've got to be. It takes a mental toll, and once you're in that cycle it's the death zone."[li]

Chapter 62

Serena

My father is undergoing an operation to fix a deviated septum. I don't go with my mother and sister to the hospital. I am so emotional when it comes to my father that I feel I need to stay home and pray for him.

Fran calls and says, "It took a long time for him to wake up, but he did regain consciousness." He comes home within a day, and has a big bandage over his nose. He doesn't look good, and I am so worried he is going to die. He eventually recovers, but it doesn't help; he still can't breathe. Intuitively I know he cannot survive another attack. About eight weeks later, my father has a doctor's appointment. He is given an oxygen tank and my mother says, "The doctor told us his blood is toxic."

The next day on February 7, 1992 I go to work. When I come home my father is sitting on a chair falling asleep. About an hour later, I go to the gym, and my father wakes up and heads to OTB, an off-track betting parlor, where he places three bets at Aqueduct Racetrack in New York. A half an hour afterward, he suffers another breathing attack. My mother says, "He was yelling to people to open up the windows," but he passes out and does not regain consciousness—this time he crosses over to the other side.

I come home, and see no one and nothing around except for some surgical gloves on the front lawn. I know he has died: I don't want to go to the hospital. I just know he is gone. I go to my Aunt Lena's house around the corner. I say, "I don't want to go to the hospital." She assures me everything is OK, but I know differently. I gather enough strength, and as I enter the medical center, my Uncle Rocco says, "You should enter this room."

My mother and sisters and my brother-in-laws are standing in this small area. I say, "He died, right?"

Mary Lou says, "He passed away." My heart drops.

I want to speak with Mary Lou, and I say, "Do you remember when I talked to you about Daddy dying?"

She says, "I don't remember."

I want to say you have to be kidding me, you don't remember? I don't say anything. I go into the room where my father is lying like a stone, and say to him, "Wherever you are, I will always love you."

I am in my brother-in-law's car, crying my eyes out as he takes me home. I am inconsolable. Then I remember that my father placed bets, and I know where he keeps his tickets. I look in my father's car and behind the sun visor are his tickets from today's races. My father has a winner in the sixth race on a horse named Roman Chorus. Chief Mistress runs second in the seventh race. He loses the late Daily Double by a nose. Chris Antley is riding in the second and third race. I don't know where he placed, as Chris is so far away from my conscious mind at this moment in time.

Sixty minutes go by as my uncle and I proceed to the funeral home. We are picking out coffins and I can't believe this is happening. My family is Catholic, and in Catholicism, the body is embalmed and laid out in front of a room. I am crying uncontrollably by his coffin, the day before we have to bury him. I'm yelling, "Wake up! I just want you to wake up."

The next day, when it is time to close the casket, I begin hyperventilating, and I scream, "I want my daddy! I want my daddy!" We bury my father on Long Island, and I am never going to see him again. I thought I was lost and empty before, but this tops the cake: my only ally in the family is now gone. I miss him so much.

Chapter 63

Serena

I am having such a hard time after my father's death. I ask Mr. O'Connell if he can do me a favor and he agrees. He asks Harvey Pack, a commentator for a horse racing show, if he will say a special thanks to a racing fan who has just passed away. It airs a week later, and I am very thankful to Mr. O'Connell and Harvey Pack for giving my father a special mention.

I thank God I am in therapy: without my therapist's guidance, I would be completely lost. She is helping me cope with my grief. Right now in therapy, I am trying to overcome my depressed state of mind, which is very difficult, as I don't fully understand my dysfunctional issues. I don't know it yet, but in time I will talk about my feelings, which is the beginning of personal transformation.

I am still trying to figure out what I want to do with my life. I quit the gym a couple of months ago to pursue other avenues. I am working part time with horses, and now I am on my own with personal training. I have a few clients and I go to their house and work them out. Now I have this idea about going to beauty school. I figure if I train people and then have skills at cutting hair, I will make a living at that. I search for a beauty school in my area, and there are two. There is one in Levittown about thirty-five minutes away, and one in Malverne about ten minutes away. I go into the European American beauty school in Malverne, and I inquire about the curriculum.

I like what I hear, and I think I will enjoy cutting and styling hair. I am talking to one of the teachers, and she is doing all the paper work to enroll me. I say, "I am a personal trainer, and I work with racehorses."

The next words out of her mouth are, "Do you know Chris Antley?"

Chapter 64

Serena

I am shocked, although I do not display any emotion. Here I am at a beauty school, with Chris Antley far away from my conscious mind. I say to myself, *I am finally over him, and now he is following me*. The teacher tells me Chris Antley's former girlfriend Kathy went to this school. She says, "Chris used to come here almost every day around two years ago."

It isn't obvious at this time, but this is a sign that Chris and I have an extraordinary connection. What are the chances that I would go to the same beauty school that he set foot in? Here I also meet a woman named Linda to whom I'm describing a situation with my mother. She says to me, "You have been hurt."

I have an "A-ha!" moment when she tells me this, and this day will stick in my mind for years to come. Yes, I am scarred, and my mother and sisters are not nice to me. I now realize that what I have to work on in therapy is my relationship with my mother.

This revelation starts me on the process of looking within. I start to spend time in bookstores: I browse the aisles, and one day I stumble into the self-help section. I pick up a book and start to read it. The written words all deal with overcoming trauma in one's life, and the material starts to resonate with me. I realize that I need to undo my dysfunctional life. I should not be looking to alter my mother's mindset, but my own.

I feel this sets me apart from most people. I want to repair myself, not someone else. I feel trying to change someone else is a waste of a lifetime. I remember what Lorelle said to me a couple of years back: "You are making a study of you."

I am on the road right now, but I feel I can be knocked off very easily. I need to regain strength from a lifetime of verbal abuse, being the scapegoat, and living life like a victim, but I am determined to proceed with my recovery.

Chapter 65

Serena

I'm off to the races to watch the Belmont Stakes in the year 1993. It's raining, and chilly for a June day in New York. Joe has a horse on today's card, and I meet him in the paddock with Mr. O'Connell as Joe's horse runs, and is out of the money (does not come in first, second or third).

Three races later is the 125th running of the Belmont Stakes. I see Hall of Famer Julie Krone, the greatest female jockey ever in the sport of racing, win the exalted race on Colonial Affair.

Right after the Belmont, a friend of mine is driving me to the airport. I am on my way to Germany. I gather up enough money to travel to the Black Forest, and board a Swiss Air flight to Zurich, Switzerland.

The flight attendant directs me to business class—how lucky am I! I arrive in Zurich after the eight-hour flight. I have some time, so I decide to stroll around before heading to the train station. I find Zurich charming, with its winding streets and beautiful architecture. After walking around the city for about an hour, I realize I should head towards the station.

I have to catch a train to a little town near Basel, Switzerland. I am a little apprehensive about traveling alone, as I don't know the language, but I am managing fine, and I meet my tour group at the Hotel Hirschen, right outside Basel. The people seem nice on this gratifying and somewhat wild but excellent adventure. We will be riding horses through the splendid dense forest and open fields of the Black Forest.

At dawn the following day, we saddle up our horses and head out for a gallop. After lunch we set out for our journey together as we enter the foothills of the Black Forest. The Black Forest consists of a thick growth of trees and pastures with small cottages along the way. I am having a great time, riding my little white German Hanoverian.

We stop for the night at the Pension Café Werny. My tour group consists of five women including myself, and two men. Most of the people are speaking Swiss-German. I am fortunate enough to have an interpreter, a woman from the Netherlands who speaks English. She is kind enough to translate for me.

The next morning at breakfast I eat the best muesli I have ever tasted. After we eat, we saddle up our horses, and are off, galloping through the lush pine forest to an old medieval castle. The castle is run-down but nonetheless amazing. This is my first trip to Europe, so everything I see is spectacular in my eyes. After marveling at the ruined castle, we jump back on our horses.

The rest of the day, the hills are alive with the sound of our horses' hooves striking earth at full speed. After we made music, we gather back at the hotel. Our horses will rest for the night at the stables. At the end of our day's ride, we enjoy some German beer. We have to rest tonight, for tomorrow we will climb to the summit of the highest mountain in the Black Forest.

It is morning and the mountains are radiant, covered with mists of dew. The sun will part the vaporous clouds very soon, and we will begin our day's journey. I eat my delicious European muesli for breakfast, and head towards the stables to saddle up my horse. We are ready to climb to four thousand feet above sea level. We start out galloping towards the natural elevation of the earth's surface.

We are at the base, and our horses proceed to climb the mountain. It is a grueling three-hour ascent, but our horses don't seem to mind it. We are almost at the crowning point, and I am so tired all I want to do was get off my horse! The group leader says, "And now we trot."

I think, *oh no, I am so tired*, but I do it and it is worth it. When I get off my horse, my leg muscles are so tight, I feel totally crippled. It takes me half an hour to recover.

The views on top of the mountain are truly gorgeous. You can see the borders of France in the distance. The richly abundant pine trees engulf this land with elaborate elegance. Germany is a shining example of our world in its splendor. Tonight, we stay at the top of the Feldberg. We rest our horses at the stables of the

Pension Wasmer. All of us are just taking in the awesome scenery that is wrapping us with joy.

On top of this divine mountain, we are going to fill our stomachs with an edible, decadent jewel. Our mouths are going to envelop layers of chocolate cake, drenched with cherry liquor and whipped cream. We inhale the appetizing scent, and now our forks are cutting into this luxury. We lift our forks to our mouths, and now we taste what is a most delicious sweet. The Black Forest cake has just left our mouths, and is traveling down into our stomachs.

After our midday pleasure, we go to our rooms to rest. Tonight we will be enjoying a great German meal. It is time for dinner, and we having traditional German food. I am having bratwurst (German sausage), and some carrots and spaetzle, a German egg noodle that I love. Dinner is over, and we go to the bar for a Black Forest drink. We are all tired, and head off to bed.

The sun is shining in my window, and I jump up and look out. I witness the parting of the mists, and the green, lush mountains appear. All of us meet in the breakfast room of our hotel and have something to eat. We are going to descend the mountain today. I navigate to the stables, where our horses have been resting. I brush my horse and put on his bridle and saddle, as we get ready for the three-hour descent. The descent is not as tiring as going up, for me or for my horse.

Three hours pass quickly, and now we are at the base of the Feldberg. We are galloping towards our last hotel, Pension Café Werny. Being with my horse in this amazing land reminds me of the Catskill Mountains of New York. My home state's peaks have the same natural landscape of this legendary forest. The best times of my childhood were in the hills where the wildcats roamed.[lii]

We arrive at the Pension, and I put my horse in his stall for the night. We head towards our rooms, as it has been a long day trotting and galloping our gorgeous horses. Hours pass and we have dinner for the last night. Tomorrow we finish our adventurous trip.

Morning arrives, and we are going over the hills and back to our original meeting point. Our horses are eager to press onward. They can sense we are heading back, and I have a strong hold on my horse. His ears are pointed upward: he is happy we are going home.

We have arrived in Basel, Switzerland, and we say good-bye to each other. It has been quite an undertaking, not knowing the language and everyone speaking Swiss-German. Riding horses through this land of fairy tales and magic has been an education for me.

I take the train to Zurich, where I will catch a flight back to New York. My experience in Germany allows me to realize that the world is so magnificent. It feels right for me to be a worldly person, one who is knowledgeable and makes a connection with this incredible earth on which we live.

Chapter 66

Serena

I am home from my amazing experience riding horses through the magical Black Forest. I ease back into the routine of working out and training people, and it is keeping me busy. When the weekends come, I have the pleasure of being around horses. My commitment to my personal growth is unwavering, and I have just joined a support group. The dysfunctional system I grew up with is becoming clearer to me.

The books I am reading resonate deep truths within me regarding what I experienced as a child. I received very few positive strokes in my childhood. I have to learn how to give myself these constructive reinforcements, which is not easy when one doesn't have any real sense of self to begin with. I am determined, and somehow I will find a solution to give myself useful feedback. First, however, I have to deal with my chronic depressed state of mind.

I am just following along with a mother who herself is depressed and didn't receive loving helpful pats on the back as a child. I learned this negative behavior and state of mind from her. I have an advantage that my mother doesn't have: I'm not blaming other people for my problems. Instead, I am looking within and asking, "What am I doing that is causing the situation?"

The month of August is here, and I am heading off to Saratoga for the weekend. I will be helping out my weekend boss, Mr. O'Connell. It is Saturday night in Saratoga Springs; the town is hopping and a friend and I are heading to a dance club. We step into the place and the DJ. is playing the "Electric Slide," so I get up and start to do the dance. Whom do I see in front of me doing the slide? Chris Antley. He has been so far away from my conscious mind, but now, here he is.

After the dance Chris and I are sitting at the same table, but he has his back towards me. Our souls are not at the forefront of this meeting, our personalities are. My personality now has a little more confidence, and I am over him, or so I think. I tap him on his shoulder and say to him, "Someone I know knows you." He responds with a nod of his head. Then I say, "One of my client's kid's eyes reminds me of you."

He echoes, "One of your client's kids," and walks away.

I am OK, not devastated like I was the last time he didn't verbally respond to me. The next thing I know, we are standing side by side again, not saying a word. Again our souls are screaming to each other, "I love you." As I am leaving the dance club, a guy I met is talking to me outside. The next thing I see is Chris leaving, running toward his car.

As Chris is leaving, my soul just wants to say "I love you," but my personality cannot. Three months later at Belmont Park, I'm standing at the rail of the racetrack, watching horses gallop for their morning workouts when I think I see Chris on a horse. The person says "Hello," to me, and I am thrilled he said, "Hello." But I find out it is not him, as Chris moved to California three weeks prior.

Chapter 67

Chris

Summer is a time of year when it's easy to be warmed by the sun's uplifting radiation. Not me: in the year 1993, I am down and out.

Life for me doesn't seem exciting anymore. I don't have an appreciation for anything. I am living, but sleepwalking at the same time. I'm in Saratoga right now, and I should be happy but I'm not.

One warm, shimmering night, I decide to step into a dance club. The place is filled with hundreds of people dancing and drinking. I hear the song "Electric Slide" playing. I know the slide, so I get up and start doing the dance and singing, "It's electric." The dance is over, and I turn around, and see my heart-pounding girl. I haven't seen her in so long. She is at the same table as me, and I have my back towards her, as I don't know what to say.

She taps me on my shoulder, and says she knows somebody that knows me. I just nod my head and then she proceeds to tell me I look like one of her client's kids. I don't know what to say to that; I think she is putting me down. I walk away from her. I think everyone hates me,[liii] especially someone that I am attracted to.

An hour passes, and I notice the girl who puts me in a trance is leaving the club with a guy. I run right past them. I feel so lonely. The next week I get suspended for rough riding—I decide to fly to California and ride, and I get suspended there too. I like the feel of the tracks here. There's nothing for me in New York anymore, so I'm considering moving to California.

Chapter 68

Chris

I book a flight on a westbound 737.

October is here, and I feel good about leaving New York at this time. I guess I'm tired of racing here. My business has been winding down. I'm not getting the mounts. I could go to Florida for the winter, like other riders. I'm going to the Breeder's Cup, so I will spend the winter in California and, if things work out, I'll stay there for good.[liv]

It's the season for a change, the time to start a brand new life. I hire a new agent, and soon I realize I don't know most of the people in California. My agent and I start to make the rounds, going into the barns getting to know the trainers. There are a lot of top jockeys here, with fewer horses to ride. California is going to be tough, but I'm up to the challenge. I have a reputation now as a person who can fly in and out of addictive states, but I am proving I can stay in the west and ride in top form.

My weight is always an issue now, so I flip (vomit) and take water pills. I don't know how long I can keep up my schedule to reduce five to seven pounds each day. For now I love the climate here in Southern California. New York's weather was really getting to me. Especially when racing moved to Aqueduct, the cold, bitter, dreary days would get me down.

At least when you have the sun shining, it brings your spirits up to some degree. I am hanging out with fellow jockey Cory Nakatami, and he is showing me around the area.[lv] In this moment in time, I am as content as I can be. How long it will stay this way I don't know. For now I am enjoying the Golden State's racing and sunshine.

Chapter 69

Serena

When I hear Chris has relocated, I say to myself, *I guess we were not meant to be together*. This is the fall of 1993. My father died last year, and now Chris is three thousand miles away. I have now become less interested in horse racing.

I am more interested in understanding myself. The road is so foggy, I can barely see the way ahead, but an inner voice is telling me to stay on this journey of self-discovery. *I am also, starting to question the collective worldview of death and beyond.*

Traveling this particular road is difficult in this society. Our world doesn't value inner personal development nor the understanding of the beyond. We are expected to follow our family, and the rules of the land.

What if our family didn't have the tools to raise their children in a healthy manner? That's what I am learning: my family didn't give me the tools to live a healthy and prosperous life. Therefore, I have to give myself the instruments for living a better life. I want to live in full abundance and fulfillment with a sense of peace and love. How do I provide myself these things?

The only way I know right now is to keep reading self-help books and stay in therapy. I have just begun on this adventure and I want to find out why I did not die in my car crash. In the midst of exploring the broken pieces of my messed-up life, I have created a personal training business. I visit people's houses to work them out, and business is thriving. It is winter in New York, and I want to escape the cold and snow for a week, I'm on my way to Cancún, Mexico.

I'm still living at home, and I tell my mother I'm going away. She throws a temper tantrum, screaming, "No you're not!" Then she calls my sisters and says, "Look at this prima donna. Who does she think she is?" Do you think I cancel my trip? No, I do not. I'm on my way to Cancún.

I'm going alone to Mexico, so I'm a little nervous, but the anxiety subsides very quickly. I'm meeting some beautiful people in Cancún. I'm staying at Club Med, an all-inclusive paradise, with lots of activities to keep one busy. I am on an excursion to visit the ancient Mayan ruins of Chichen Itza—by plane! The plane has just landed, and some people I met from Club Med are boarding a bus to the ancient site. We arrive, and I see an ancient pyramid in the distance. The pyramid is very steep but doesn't look that hard to climb. I am right, and it takes me about twenty minutes to reach the summit.

The sun is so hot, but I'm almost at the peak. I make it to the highest point, and a hair-raising view greets me at the zenith. At this site in ancient times, the Mayans played a game, sort of like basketball today. What I learn piques my interest: the winner is sacrificed, so that he can reincarnate and come back to earth again.

At this time I'm extremely ignorant about the ancient people called the Mayans. I did not realize that they were a very advanced civilization in their time. They were aware of a very important date: one of their calendars ends on December 21, 2012, so this day holds great meaning. The Mayans believe a change in our worldview will be ushered in around December 21, 2012.

I arrive back at my tropical oasis, and in a few days I will leave this heavenly spot. The time to depart has come, and I had a fabulous time in Mexico. I learned a lot about our world, and had fun in the sun.

I am back home, and it's spring. I have a goal now to move out of my mother's house by the summer. A couple of months have passed since I set my goal. I'm at a family party and I see one of my personal belongings in my cousin's house. I start to scream at my mother, and I ask her, "Who gave you the right to give away my stuff?"

She says, "You didn't need it."

The next day, I visit a real estate agent, determined to find my own apartment. I feel grateful I'm in a position to move out of my mother's house. I'm twenty-eight years old, and I am leaving for good. I relocated at eighteen, and moved back in with my parents at twenty-one. I feel the time is right to be on my own, and I rent an apartment in Long Beach, New York. I will be living alone in my own space with my dog Romeo.

Chapter 70

Chris

The California sunshine is persuading me to put down roots in the west.

It has been a little over a year since I made the move from New York. I like it here, and I have been riding some good horses. However, I cannot stand dropping weight every day. I don't know how much longer I can take it. In order for me to make weight, I have to go through the fires of hell.

Five full moons come and go, and I am inching my way towards drugs and alcohol again. I don't see anything optimistic about my life. I'm withdrawn, and I don't value myself. I have been dating a girl here, and we break up. I might ride a couple of times a day if I'm lucky. I am spiraling out of control, and today I'm taking off from riding. I feel better when I'm on drugs.

The 1995 Kentucky Derby is upon us, and I am on a horse named In Character. We are off and running. I see the filly Serena's Song has the speed and is leading. My horse has nothing in him, and we are in the back of the pack, finishing tenth, behind the eventual winner Thunder Gulch with my friend Gary Stevens in the irons.

I do not have any mounts in the Preakness and Belmont Stakes and as weeks pass, I decide to check into rehab for the umpteenth time to see if I can pull myself together. I am going to try to transform myself, but it is not easy. I need a sense of security within, and all I have is admiration coming from the outside.

I'm an awakened soul with an inferior personality and a divine talent. I don't know how to get a sense of safety; maybe I need to go back to South Carolina, and see if I can find this elusive trait. I want to keep riding. What will I do if I go home? For now I'm in California, in rehab, trying to stay clean and sober.

Chapter 71

Serena

I feel free, living in my own space. My personal training business is prospering, and I am focused on looking within. The self-help books are helping me understand myself.

Some months ago I was watching the Kentucky Derby. Serena's Song, owned by Bob and Beverly Lewis and trained by Wayne Lukas, was leading until the top of the stretch. She faded, and was out of the money. I fall in love with the name Serena—I think it is very beautiful. Now, I have detached myself from horse racing, and have stopped working on the weekends at Belmont Park. It's a whole new life I have created for myself, and it feels good.

The court case about my car accident comes to a close, and I receive some money from the settlement. Life is good at this moment in time. One day I am flipping through a magazine, and I see an advertisement: *Come to Egypt on a Life, Death, and Beyond Conference at the Pyramids of Giza. James van Praagh, the psychic medium is going to be joining us.* I see the ad, and it entices me to inquire about the tour. I call the phone number and speak with a representative. I just booked my trip to Egypt. I've always wanted to go to this ancient country, and now I am on my way!

Six months later, at the age of twenty-nine, I venture off into the sunset. I'm on an Air Egypt flight from New York to Cairo. I am traveling alone again, but I'm on a spiritual journey with like-minded people. There will be a group of speakers presenting their stories on their near-death experiences. Some of the people from the tour are here on the plane. During the flight I am talking to one woman, a psychic she said, "I can bring you into a meditative state and raise your soul from your body." I take her up on her offer and she brings me into an altered state. Immediately, I feel faint. She said, "That is your soul rising out of your body!"

The plane has landed, and I take one step on the soil of this age-old land, and I know I am home. I arrive in Cairo at night, and the hotel car service picks me up at the airport. Forty-five minutes pass, and I arrive at The Mena House.

The Mena House overlooks the pyramids, and I requested a room with a view months ago. I check in, and take the elevator up to my room, which I will be sharing with another person from the group. I look out the window, but I just see total darkness. I glide downstairs to the front desk and I say, "I requested a room overlooking the pyramids and I don't seem to be in such a place." The person assures me I have a grand view of the pyramids.

I proceed back to my room, and a couple of minutes later, I see one of the pyramids in all its glory. These colossal formations are illuminated with bright light every twenty minutes. That's why I couldn't see anything: first there was darkness; then there was light. I am in awe, and scream with such intensity, "Oh my God!" I simply cannot believe my eyes. I am blown away by the powerful mystic force these immortal structures convey.

I will be staying at the hotel for the week. I am attending meditation classes, and listening to different speakers on their near-death encounters. One woman died for an hour and a half, and survived to tell about her experience. James Van Praagh cancelled at the last minute, and the tour asked Marianne Williamson to take James Van Praagh's place.

I have so much energy. I cannot believe I am here. I am so elated to be in Egypt that I keep looking up at the sky, as I am feeling close to the Divine. One morning Nancy, Dina (two girls I become friends with), and I wake up at 4:30 a.m. and take a taxi to a stable behind the pyramids. Arabian horses are in their stalls, and camels are lying down outside of the barns. The three of us climb on top of our camels. My camel leans forward to get up. The camel and I have risen.

We are walking, and we proceed to trek towards the pyramids in the darkness of the early morning. A light is shining in the blackness, as the full moon is piercing the veil of a light mist. Twenty minutes go by, and I witness a mesmerizing event.

The sun is starting to come up over the horizon, as it has done for thousands of years, by the unimaginable, awe-inspiring Pyramids of Giza.

Dawn's early light is chasing away the full moon. The sky is swirling with pale clouds infused with vivid tints of pink and purple. The sands of the Sahara are engulfing me with a magical gift of love for our world. The richness of this ancient land is awakening my soul to a long-past memory. The pebbles of the desert are intoxicating me with feelings that are overwhelming, knowing that a part of me has been here before.

Very quickly I am brought back to the here and now. As Ra was glowing bright all day, twilight is approaching. A group of us are driving to a restaurant down the road from the hotel. We are gathering in two cars; I am already delegated to one vehicle but head to the other car to tell someone that the bellhops here have the same hats as Uncle Haji from the TV show *I Dream of Jeannie*.

I am now in the other car, and we get to the restaurant, but some of us don't like what is being served. So we hop into another taxi when a few feet ahead of us… a man is in the middle of the road. The man is telling the taxi driver, "Everyone has to get out: they are killing Egyptians." We leave the taxi and now we are in the middle of chaos—machine guns are firing, gun smoke is everywhere.

The people of Egypt didn't like who was elected, and three people were killed in this mess. Within minutes we get into another taxi and are led into the back entrance of the hotel passing men with half-cocked machine guns ready to fire. Needless to say, this is a very scary situation.

The moment passes and during the week we get the chance to have a unique experience inside one of the pyramids. Each night a different speaker leads a group through the interior of the Great Pyramid. I will be meditating between 11:00 p.m. and 1:00 a.m., when the site is closed to the public. Marianne Williamson, a fabulous spiritual teacher, leads us, and the experience is orgasmic. I am tapping into a state of oneness with myself and the world.

Five sunsets have passed, and it is my last day in Egypt. While most of my tour goes on to different parts of the country, I stay behind and hire a tour guide for a few hours. I will be sharing the cost with Dina, as we will be exploring Cairo. The smell of Cairo enchants me with its burning of garbage. Palm trees are undulating in the warm air, and people in their cars are honking their horns to let other vehicles know to get out of the way.

First we stop and explore the Egyptian Museum. Ancient Egypt's past has been scattered throughout the world in different museums, but the Egyptian Museum houses King Tutankhamen's main treasures. The building also has a temperature-controlled mummy room where Ramses II, and Queen Hatshepsut are housed.

Next, we stop where Moses is said to have been found by the River Nile. Seeing the site is very special to me. I am becoming more and more intrigued with Moses while I am here. We have a great day, and then head back to the hotel.

Dina and I are by the pyramids for the last time. She says, "Can you feel the energy that is radiating from these stones?" I agree I feel an electrifying force. She says, "It is nice to be able to sense energy, and have someone else perceive it too and not think that you are crazy." Dina, who is from Malta, and I will be having an early dinner. Tomorrow both of us are heading home. I think we can both agree Egypt has been an experience we will never forget.

Chapter 72

Chris

Rehab is calling me again in the year 1996.

The 1996 Kentucky Derby has come and gone, as I rode a horse named Louis Quatorze to a sixteenth-place finish. I am taken off of him in the Preakness, and jockey Pat Day guides Louis Quatorze home and gets the victory. I am trying to recover from a life of drug use. As for my career, I will be in and out of horse racing for the rest of my life.

Rehab feels safe, and I understand I need to develop my security within, but I just don't seem to have the skills to do it. Having money in the bank doesn't give me emotional security. Cash is security at one level in life, but material wealth can't give me self-worth or an identity. *I'm reading quite a number of self-help and spiritual books, and I am trying to incorporate the knowledge into my life. Some books speak of the soul, and I start to understand the depth of me.*

I am gaining weight here in rehab, and it is very frustrating. That means once I leave, I will have to start the whole process of reducing. I hate that I have to watch the scale. I want to eat what I want, and not have to flip. I don't have that luxury at all in my life. If I want to continue riding in this game of horse racing, I have to deal with the torture of making weight.

I am able to sleep late here and I could get used to it. I don't know if I will have the motivation to get up early as I used to, and go haggle for mounts. Sometimes I wonder if I should go back at all. This is all I have ever known. What would I do with my life? I don't have a clue.

My agent Ron Anderson says I can do things no one else could. He describes me to a reporter this way: "Chris has *a sixth sense* and only a handful get to that level. Horses that are lazy and don't want to run, he could make run. An extreme talent. Not good. Great."[lvi]

I know I have a gift, that I ride racehorses like no one else. However, I am filled with fear, guilt, and shame. My life is a fight against myself, and I don't know how to find peace and serenity.

Chapter 73

Serena

I'm home from my life-changing trip to Egypt, and I feel elated physically, emotionally, and spiritually. *Since my father's death, I have been questioning the collective worldview on death and beyond. It doesn't make sense to me we are here for a short period of time and, that's it? Also, the collective view of the soul is embodied in the material world. Chris and I were waking each other to the spiritual world, but I am not fully conscious yet of our eternal connection.*

However, I just came out of Egypt and experienced the flavor of my eternal nature. I have become awakened to something very profound. I tasted my immortal being rising up within and looking me in the eye, and I now have a deep urge to convert to Judaism.

After encountering this ancient land, I feel a deep affinity to Moses and what he accomplished in his life. Moses heard his everlasting soul speak to him many moons ago. He led groups of people out of Egypt into the Sinai desert where they formed a new thought system.

Just like Moses, I can feel what it is like to be one with my enduring spirit, as a wise intelligence has invaded my body with divine light. I want to emulate Moses, so I make my first step and inquire about converting to Judaism. I call up the nearest Conservative temple in Long Beach and speak with the rabbi. I will be going to temple every Saturday (The Holy Sabbath) and taking classes for the next year. The Torah (the Old Testament), which I read in English, has on almost every page the spiritual insights on what Moses is doing or has done. I feel I am following my soul and my purpose for why I am here on Earth.

Chapter 74

Serena

Every Saturday I attend temple and pray. It feels right to me that I am pursuing this change from Catholicism to Judaism. I am at home reading the Old Testament and the accomplishments Moses has made in his life. In September, I start conversion classes, which consist of learning about the history of the Jewish people.

Right now it is the peak of summer, and I'm on my way back to Egypt. I will be taking a Nile River cruise adventure. This time I want to experience the whole of Egypt. It's raining like cats and dogs in New York, and I am on an Air France plane from New York to Paris. The flight is delayed two hours because of the weather in New York. I land in Paris late and miss my connecting flight to Cairo.

Air France books me on a flight to Egypt from another airport in Paris. My suitcase is going to be on the next flight out of Charles De Gaulle Airport. I am not happy and try to explain to the people at Air France I'm going on a cruise and I probably will not get my luggage out on the Nile. I'm wasting time talking with the staff of Air France. I need to get on a shuttle bus to Orly airport in Paris, to catch my plane to Cairo.

I arrive at Orly on time and make my connecting flight. I land in Cairo in the evening, and for this tour I need to get to my hotel on my own. It's late at night, and I grab a taxi with two men from Australia. I am really nervous to be a woman alone with three men as the cab driver drops the two men off first and then me. I am relieved I make it to my hotel in one piece. I sleep like a baby and the next morning I meet my tour at breakfast.

After enjoying a cup of coffee, a few slices of meat, and a croissant, we hop on a bus and head out to the pyramids. It is so hot, and there are lots of people walking, I don't get off the bus. I had such a unique experience months ago meditating inside the pyramids, I don't want to replace that memory with anything else. The tour leaves the pyramids, and heads to the Cairo Museum and then to old Cairo. My luggage hasn't come yet, so I have to buy a few items since I have nothing to wear.

The sun is high in the sky the following afternoon when my bag finally arrives. My suitcase arrives just in time as we are boarding an overnight train from Cairo to Aswan. The train is cool, and we will be sleeping on little folding beds. My group is mostly from New Zealand and Australia, and we are in one of the cars getting to know one another. I am not satisfied with the food on the train, which is horrible.

Morning is here as I look out my window, and a haze is enveloping the air as we have arrived in Aswan, Egypt. I feel I need a shower but will not be able to take one until later. We exit the train and explore Aswan, the city by the River Nile. I step into the Cataract Hotel where Agatha Christie was inspired to write her famous novel *Death on the Nile.* The view is magnificent from the Cataract, palm trees are rocking, and the River Nile is glowing. Someone from the group shouts, "It's great to be alive." I totally agree; I am so fortunate to be here.

We head to our hotel, and I am so glad to take a shower. Nighttime falls upon us, as we are bicycling around town. After experiencing beautiful Aswan, we eat dinner at the hotel, and I'm off to bed early.

A 3:00 a.m. wakeup call is here, as we are in for a three-hour bus ride. We are driving to the border of Egypt and Sudan (Nubian territory). The bus is taking us to the majestic temple of Abu Simbel, which glorifies its constructor, Pharaoh Ramses II. The four colossal statutes of Pharaoh Ramses II are seven stories high. Abu Simbel is supposed to be dedicated to the trinity of gods: solar king of the gods, Amon-Ra, solar god, Horakhty, and creator god, Ptah. In truth it is mainly dedicated to Ramses II.

This creation was not just about fabricating an esteemed structure for the glory of Ramses. The Egyptians dominated the ancient Nubians but wanted to overpower their economy. Building Abu Simbel was a statement to the Nubians from the Egyptians: Look what we can do, and don't come any farther into our territory.

Being here is hypnotic. The floods of the River Nile were diverted to form Lake Nasser. The glistening body of water flows right beside these enormous, impressive statues of Ramses. Lake Nasser sparkles like diamonds, as the sun shines his light. It is as if I am put into a trance by something higher than my ego. Through these enchanting experiences, I am realizing my true nature. On an unconscious level I am remembering my eternal core has experienced this before. There is a sense of familiarity in this country my soul knows so well. I am in a state of euphoria at Abu Simbel. I perceive a close bond to my everlasting being and the Divine. This feeling transcends my whole way of knowing the world.

As we are driving back from Abu Simbel to Aswan, I turn my head to the left and I see what looks like water but isn't. I am witnessing my first desert mirage. We arrive in Aswan in the early afternoon, and now are boarding a riverboat. A three-day journey up the River Nile to Luxor is waiting for us. Floating up the River Nile is a breathtaking experience. By the river's edge there are exquisite date palms that just make you stare with delight. I wish I could capture this moment forever.

The riverboat has docked, and my group and I enter a unique temple complex. This fascinating site is dedicated to the solar god Horus and to the crocodile god Sobek. Kom Ombo was built during the Greco-Roman period of Egyptian history. We head back for some afternoon tea. After tea I relax by the ship's pool, enjoying the atmosphere. Dusk is upon us, and I decide to take a walk. I stop and watch a snake charmer hypnotize her reptile into submission.

I realize it's time for dinner and head back to meet my group. The full moon shines bright in the sky and we enjoy eating dinner outside on the upper deck of the boat. Being on the Nile, the full moon perhaps fuels my attraction to our handsome tour leader, and I experience an amazing sexual encounter with the dirty-blond-haired, blue-eyed, British guide.

The next day feels very surreal as we get off the boat and head to the Valley of the Kings. In the old and middle kingdoms of ancient Egypt, kings were buried in pyramids. At the beginning of the new kingdom (1550–1069 BC), kings were buried on the west bank of the Nile, in the Valley of the Kings.

It is so hot! The temperature is over a hundred degrees, with very little shelter. The only respite is going down into the burial sites. The most famous tomb belongs to King Tutankhamen, better known as King Tut. King Tut's tomb was found in the 1920s and most of his treasures are in the Cairo Museum. His mummified body is kept here, with a twenty-four-hour guard on watch. After viewing his tomb, everyone heads back to the boat and relaxes by the pool.

I am in heaven. I'm so relaxed, and it feels peaceful being on the Nile. Tonight, I am going to spend the last night on the river getting dressed up in ancient Egyptian attire. Everyone has a great time at the party, dancing the Macarena and drinking wine. The next day we all disembark, and will spend the next two nights in Luxor, Egypt.

It is late afternoon on another gorgeous hot day in Egypt, and we are trekking to the great Karnak Temple. The main building of Karnak is devoted to the god Amun. The sacred hallway lined with immense mystical pillars connects to the sanctuary, and is a brilliant example of Egyptian architecture at its finest.

These massive columns stand seventy-six feet high, and are fifty feet in circumference. I am captivated by these stupendous pillars. One of the people in the group faints because she is dehydrated, but she soon recovers. Afterward, everyone goes back to the hotel and gets ready for dinner. I am hanging out by the pool with a few people from the group. We are in Luxor, Egypt, but in ancient times Luxor was called Thebes. The next morning we trek to the middle of the city to the Temple of Luxor.

An avenue of sphinxes connects Luxor to Karnak, two miles to the north. The main purpose of Luxor was to host an annual festival, which led the images of the gods to Karnak by land and by boat. As I am walking through the complex, and marveling at these ancient ruins, it feels like I'm having an out-of-body experience. It's awe-inspiring to be among such artifacts of early history. I spend the rest of the day relaxing by the pool. It's the last night that everyone is together. Tomorrow some people are going onto another destination. I experience another great night with Dave, the handsome tour leader. The next day is here, and we are heading to the airport. We have a stopover in Kuwait and then we're on to Cairo.

We arrive in Cairo in one piece, and actually have time to go to the famous bazaar. I shop for a few items: the usual tee shirts, trinkets, and the like. This is my last night in Egypt, and I discover that two of the girls on the tour are jealous of me, as they had wanted to be with the tour leader, when instead he chose to be with me. I wasn't consciously aware at the time that I was being envied, but I know it doesn't feel good to me. I'm having a sad moment, having to say goodbye to Dave and Egypt. Tomorrow I'm on a flight back to New York.

Chapter 75

Serena

I felt alive and free being in the mystical land of the Pharaohs. My sexual encounter with the British tour leader was a spicy adventure, and I didn't want it to end. Now I am home and lonely. I am not doing too well emotionally. I should be fulfilled. I am not living in the abusive household with my mother. Now the work begins, as I will need to find the power to overcome the dysfunction.

My conversion classes begin in a few weeks, and I am looking forward to them. A few days ago I received a phone call from a guy I met on my trip to Martinique. He said he is coming to New York City and asked if I'd like to meet up with him. I said yes, and I drive into the city and meet Mike at a hotel.

Mike and I and a couple of his friends are hanging out for the night. I make plans to hook up with one guy the next week. We go on a date and it is OK, so I start to date him. We go out for a few months, and then we mutually break it off. I am fine with the decision, as I know he is not the one for me.

I am now in the traveling mood, so I book a trip to London, Amsterdam, and Paris. I will be going on a tour, and I invite Nancy, a friend whom I met in Martinique, to come. We will be leaving on December 26, 1996. I will be in Amsterdam, Netherlands for New Year's Eve.

≈

Chapter 76

Serena

Nancy and I are on our way to England. A British Airways flight is transporting us from New York to London. We arrive in the United Kingdom on a nippy, dreary day and are supposed to meet our tour tomorrow. We take a taxi to our hotel and check into our room. Nancy is tired, and all she wants to do is go to sleep.

I want to explore London, and I become annoyed that she wants to waste time resting. I decide to plunge ahead on my own and explore the city. I stumble onto Hyde Park and I witness as the phenomenon of Speaker's Corner, where people come to express their opinions. People gather around, listening to whatever other people have to say. I find it to be very inspiring that anyone can go there and articulate their feelings or opinions.

The British Museum is calling me, and I find my way to this cultural landmark. The first section I visit is the Egyptian collection. This museum houses the Rosetta Stone, unearthed in the 1700s. It is through the discovery of this block of knowledge that mankind can now decipher the ancient Egyptian language. After my wanderings, I venture back to the hotel to check on my friend, and she is still sleeping. About an hour passes and she finally wakes up. I ask her, "Why did you come on this trip?"

She says, "To have a good time."

We skip to the lobby of the hotel, and I see a poster. The poster says: *Join us on the Jack the Ripper Tour tonight.* I say to myself, I would really like to do that and ask Nancy if she would like to go. She says, "I might be interested," but she isn't, and I go by myself. The tour starts at eight in the evening. There are about ten people in the group, and they take us on a stroll around the streets of London. We stop where Mr. Jack murdered his victims, and at the end we gather in a pub for some fish and chips and beer.

Most of us go our separate ways, but I meet a couple of people who are staying at my hotel. We walk back together, and hang out at the bar downstairs. I venture upstairs to check on Nancy, who is still sleeping, so I go back downstairs and continue to have a good time. The next day Nancy and I meet our tour, and we're on our way to Buckingham Palace, Westminster Abbey, and Big Ben.

We are outside of Buckingham Palace on a sunny but freezing cold day, waiting for the changing of the guards. Finally after an hour, the guards, who are standing for eight hours in front of the historic building, switch roles with new men. After seeing the royal routine, Nancy and I and the group head to the biggest clock in the world, Big Ben. Somehow I become separated from Nancy, and I start to hang out with a couple of other girls. We explore the Tower of London, and we want to see the Crown Jewels. I am so frozen, and it is a thirty-minute wait to get to the door. I say to myself, *I am not going to make it*, and start to do jumping jacks and run in place—I warm myself up by doing thirty minutes of cardio.

Once I am in the museum I am astonished by the gorgeous pieces of jewelry on display belonging to the royal family. There are emeralds, diamonds, and rubies galore. My new friends, Hanna and Marcy, and I are now taking a bus to Harrods, the famous store, for some afternoon tea—lots of fun, and the thing to do in London. We then go back to the hotel and I meet up with Nancy, who says she didn't come along since she was tired.

I don't have the capacity to see that my personality on this trip becomes identified with my opposite. I become centered on my outgoing persona, and am thinking about my needs as opposed to always focusing on others. At this time in my life, this side of me has not yet been fully integrated into my personality.

I also do not have the insight to see that my independent nature is hard for people to accept. I guess Nancy wanted me to stay with her, but I went off on my own. I am acting narcissistic at this moment, and I am thinking about only myself. My personality identifies with the empress, as I just want to have a good time. I do not own the monarch mentality, and I attract Marcy into my life. Later, I will discover she is a mirror image of my mother: mean and competitive. For tonight, all of us are going to a London pub.

We are having a great time drinking, eating, and laughing. Tomorrow we are off to Amsterdam.

The next day is here, and I have coffee and eggs for breakfast. An hour passes, and then we hop onto our bus. We are driving towards the ocean so we can board a ferry. The ship will be crossing the English Channel and heading to the Netherlands. I make my way to the top deck of the boat, and I stay out there for a moment. The water is rough, and the clouds are low in the sky on this chilly day at sea. I snap a picture of the channel and head inside. Three hours have passed, and the ferry has now docked in the Netherlands.

We jump onto our bus and head to the city of Amsterdam. We arrive at nightfall and set out to explore the red light district. This side of town is famous for its pubs that sell marijuana cigarettes. The sale of the funny cigarette is not legal in the Netherlands, but it is tolerated. None of my friends venture into any of the bars though. The next day is New Year's Eve, and we are spending the night at the hotel. All of us are ringing in the New Year with a sense of happiness and delight.

New Year's Day all of us have a hangover. Most places of interest are closed for the holiday, so the tour leader takes us to an old fishing village just outside of the city. It is sunny but extremely cold, and we enter a cheese factory to get out of the wintery weather. People dressed in old-fashioned attire (long dresses and clogs) show us around, and graciously offer us some wine and cheese.

The cold winds of Europe blow into the evening of New Year's Day, and we gather at a Chinese restaurant in Amsterdam. This is the first time I hear police sirens on this continent and it's freaking me out. The sirens are the same as they were in the Nazi era. Thinking of the Nazis reminds me that the Anne Frank house is closed for the holiday—a couple of people and I want to visit the famous site before we go to Paris, France.

The next day Mel, Lisa, and I go on our own to the Anne Frank house. We are going to meet up with our tour in Brussels, Belgium and then head to Paris. We enter the house of Anne Frank, and right away I'm transported back in time. It baffles me that eight people were hiding from the Nazis in such a tiny apartment. Inside the rooms the air is frigid, just like it was in

Anne's day. If anyone doesn't know the story, the Nazis discover Anne and her family are hiding in this apartment. In August 1944, the Nazis arrest Anne and her family and bring them to concentration camps; everyone is killed except Anne's father. Anne's diary survives this tragic event, and we have her wisdom for all of humanity to read for years to come. It is such an emotional experience. I am glad I was able to visit this historic place.

My friends and I are on our way to the train station to catch a train to Brussels and meet our tour. We are on the train when all of a sudden it stops, and is suspended for quite some time. The conductor informs us that we cannot go any farther because of icy rails. They are diverting us to Antwerp. We are OK with the situation, and will have to get to Paris on our own. At this time, cell phones are not as common as today, so we don't have a way to contact our tour leader. We just say, "When they see we are not at the meeting place, they will figure out we are going to get to Paris on our own." We arrive at the Antwerp train station, and purchase a ticket to Paris. As we are waiting, I buy a Belgium waffle: with little bits of sugar hidden inside, it is especially delicious. The train to Paris will take around three hours. Once we are there, we'll take a taxi to our hotel.

We arrive at the hotel about a half an hour sooner than our tour! Everyone wants to know what happened to us. They all think it was a fabulous escapade, and I agree. We settle into our hotel room, and Nancy says she knew I was all right. She said I have "an adventurous spirit." A couple of hours later our tour is at the Eiffel Tower. While we are on the bus, the tour leader puts on Duran Duran's song, "A View to a Kill." *A View to a Kill* is also a James Bond movie involving horse racing. At the start of the film Mr. Bond is chasing someone up the Eiffel Tower, while the Duran Duran song plays in the background.

We cannot climb the tower because it is closed, but marvel at this awesome structure from the ground. The rest of the evening, the bus drives us around the city of lights, showing us the major points. The next day all of us are going to the Louvre Museum. I am so ignorant about art at this point of my life, but I can appreciate looking at the famed *Mona Lisa* and the *Venus de Milo.* For me, visiting this prestigious museum is an introduction to the world of art. After the Louvre we experience Napoleon's tomb and Notre Dame Cathedral. The day is dismal and ice-cold, but exploring these well-known sites fascinates me.

The darkness of night is here, and all of us eat at a stylish Parisian restaurant. After dinner, we are on our way to the Moulin Rouge. The Moulin Rouge is a musical show that today entertains tourists, but played only to male clients back in the day. I think the show is OK, nothing to brag about. Now we are heading back to our hotel for a drink at the bar. Even Nancy is up and having a drink with us. We end the night on a good note.

We welcome in the next day with breakfast as we pack up our belongings and load our suitcases onto the bus. We have a long way to go before we're back in London. We will go on the ferry again and then onto our hotel. We arrive in London around seven o'clock in the evening. For our last night together, we gather at a pub where we eat fish and chips and drink beer. All of us are having a great time and discussing our adventure. I am attracted to the tour leader, but we don't get together. I make connections with three people on this trip: two of them live in Pennsylvania, and the third lives in New York.

I am not sure if I will stay in contact with Nancy. We were hardly together the entire trip. She was hanging out with a guy from Miami, and I was hanging out with new friends. Nevertheless, I feel both Nancy and I had an amazing experience across Europe.

Chapter 77

Chris

I am discharged from the rehabilitation center in early 1997.

I finish my drug rehab program, and feel I need to fly to South Carolina to ride in the Ellorree trails. This is a day when horses from all over come and compete in my hometown. I make a promise to my friend Mr. Smith, who had confidence in me before I believed in myself. Mr. Smith knew I would be a star rider.

I tell him I want to make the Ellorree trails more of an event and that I will bring people to South Carolina in the future. Mr. Smith knows I would never forget my roots. He later tells a reporter, "Everyone around this community kept up with Chris's career and asked about him all the time."[lvii]

When I hear this, I say, "Tell them I thank them very much."

A few months later I hear an old friend needs a job. Drew just got fired by a jockey he was handling, so I meet with him, and before we know it we are hugging each other. Going forward, Drew will be handling my book for me.

Drew remembers when we first met: I was a small town country kid and he was a city slicker. Our first encounter with each other didn't go smoothly, as he thought I was too cocky. Within a few weeks Drew looked deeply into me and saw my vulnerability. I have to thank Drew for dealing with the part of my personality that comes out when I'm on drugs. I had to hide that side of myself from my family, and be the good boy my mother wanted.

I will have to ride in New York again, and before I know it I am flying on a plane, ready to touch down in the Big Apple. It is now May of 1997. I have rented my house that I own on Long Island, so I'll be staying with Drew and his family.

Chapter 78

Serena

Nancy and I are home after our wonderful trip from Europe. We say goodbye to each other at the airport. I have my car parked at my mother's house, and I get there by taxi. My mother is taking care of Romeo while I am away. It is late, around nine o'clock in the evening on a Sunday. I scheduled clients bright and early the next day. I get into my car but when it doesn't start, I panic. I run to a gas station a block away to see if they can help me, but it's closed.

I call up roadside assistance, and the Mitsubishi people come around an hour later and jump my battery. My mother needles me, saying, "You think about going away? See what happens? You need to think about the practical things in life."

I don't pay attention, but the sting is there. She is not happy seeing me in high spirits. I get home around midnight and I am exhausted and fall right to sleep. I get up the next day feeling renewed excitement, remembering I had such a great time on my trip.

About two weeks later, I call Nancy and tell her I'm going to New Orleans with the two girls I met on the trip. I don't think she is too pleased with that, and I never hear from her again. I'll be flying to New Orleans in May, but for right now I'm focusing on converting to Judaism.

For the past eight months I've been going to temple every Saturday and have been attending classes every week. I am on my way to the Beth Din, which is a group of five or six rabbis who are invested in religious matters. I have to stand before the rabbis, stating why I want to convert to Judaism.

I enter the room, and the rabbis are around a big conference table. One of the rabbis asks me to go to the bookshelf and pick out a book, so I go to the shelf and pick out a novel about the origins of Judaism. The rabbis are very impressed with my choice and say, "You are making a decision that is very deep." I pass the test and now have one more ritual to do before I am fully converted. I have to submerge myself in the Mikvah, which is like a small swimming pool of holy waters.

I drive about forty minutes on the Long Island Expressway to Commack, New York. I meet some of the girls in my class at the temple. Most people convert to Judaism because they are marrying someone of the Jewish faith. I am changing because I want to feel closer to my own soul.

When I tell one of my sisters what I was doing, she is highly offended, but I tell her I have to do what my soul wishes. I step into the holy waters naked and a rabbi stands around the bend so he can't see. I have to recite a prayer in Hebrew, and then the rabbi says I am Jewish! In the course of the conversion, I have had to pick a Hebrew name.

I want to be named *Ahava,* which means love. One of the rabbis says, "*Ahava* is not a name," so he gave me the name *Ahova,* which means the beloved. I will continue to go to temple every Saturday, and pray to the divine energy of the universe. I feel great that I converted, and now I am planning to go to Israel in the summer. I'm looking forward to making a pilgrimage to the biblical land, but in a couple of weeks I will be going to New Orleans with the friends I made in Europe.

Chapter 79

Serena

The city of New Orleans is waiting for the arrival of Hanna, Marcy, and me. We are on a US Airways flight, and we land in New Orleans around midday. My friends and I are staying in the French Quarter. I am in the United States, but this part of town has an old European feel.

We check into our hotel to freshen up and then take a taxi across town. It's raining but we are committed to an Anne Rice tour. We visit Anne Rice's old, white Victorian house with its beautiful landscaped gardens. The author of the famed vampire books is a native of New Orleans. After the tour we are hungry and venture into a restaurant to have some Cajun food. I order some popcorn shrimp, and we all have a delicious meal and proceed to get the check. Marcy and I are figuring out the bill, when all of a sudden Marcy just snaps.

She yells, "Don't tell me what each of us needs to put in. How dare you to tell me what to do?"

I am mortified. I don't know why what I just said ("Each of us needs to contribute eleven dollars,") would cause her to go ballistic. Marcy is degrading me, and I don't say anything. She is acting like my mother: mean and domineering. Once again, I am the scapegoat and take the blame for the bullies in my life. It's not until years after this event that I will understand I have attracted a narcissistic friend. What I need to learn is how to stand up to such people.

This situation is not good for me. I immediately take the blame for my friend's intimidating tactic. As we are walking back to the hotel, and even though I am right there, Marcy tells Hanna, "I can't take her crap," as if I can't hear. We proceed to our room and I am about to leave, when Marcy says something else, and I say with tears in my eyes, "What was that about?"

I take the elevator downstairs. I sit by the hotel pool, asking myself what I am doing here. I am supposed to be in Turkey, but my trip was cancelled. Reluctantly I head back, and Marcy pretends she is sick, so Hanna and I hang out alone for the rest of the night.

The next day the sun is shining in our hotel room. Marcy and I make up, and the rest of the trip goes smoothly. We get up early and take a cab to the swampy waters of New Orleans. New Orleans is surrounded by rivers, lakes, and the bayou. It is raining, but we get on a boat anyway. Spanish moss is everywhere, hanging from tree to tree, and I see an alligator and then another. Our tour around the marshland takes around an hour; then we are off to our hotel for a rest. We are sitting in our room talking, and Hanna and Marcy want to do something I'm not interested in doing, so I tell them I'll go on the Mississippi cruise, and we can meet up in a couple of hours.

They say, "No problem!" and we do our own thing. It really wasn't OK with them. It will be years before I find out from Marcy she was not happy I left them. She says, "You just can't go off on your own." I am shocked. She had Hanna with her; did she really need me? Certainly not, but I am expressing a part of myself that she cannot express. So instead of realizing it is her own problem, she makes it my issue.

We have one more day in this great southern city, and we are off to an old plantation. We take a bus to Grand Oak Alley, a historic piece of land between New Orleans and Baton Rouge, Louisiana. The Greek-style mansion is located on the Mississippi River. As you enter the territory, the quarter-mile road, lined with live oak trees, mesmerizes you. These colossal, supreme oaks drape over the road leading up to the estate, and they are believed to be three hundred years old. I am captivated by the terrain and majestic trees of this very old piece of land. Hanna, Marcy, and I have a great time wandering around the grounds. We head back towards downtown New Orleans. We spend our last night eating and drinking on the famed Bourbon Street. Tomorrow we have an early flight to New York.

While I am in New Orleans, I start to think about Chris Antley. I don't know why, until I look in the newspaper when I get home and see he is once again riding in New York. I think, *I must be psychic when it comes to him*, not consciously realizing yet that our souls are connected. I don't think twice about this, and sail on with my life!

Chapter 80

Chris

Spring is in the air, and the trees are budding with new life. The April showers have ended and May flowers are ready to bloom. I am riding at Belmont Park.

I am living in Garden City with Drew his wife and their kids, and I feel happy being part of a family. I have struggled emotionally, not knowing where I belong, but I feel secure being around loving people. I love playing with Drew's children, as it makes me want to become a child again.

My friend Nick Zito is very optimistic about putting me on his horses, and the other trainers I used to regularly ride for seem optimistic as well. I am doing my best to keep my weight down, but it is not easy: every day is like climbing a mountain. I am here, and I don't see the girl who put me in a trance. I bet she is married with kids by now. I stop in the stores and restaurants I used to frequently visit, and it feels like I never left New York.

The end of July is upon us, and I am looking forward to Saratoga Springs again. I can't wait to ride and live at the Spa (a name referring to the mineral springs of Saratoga) for six weeks. About twenty-one days into the meet, I have a horse break down while I am riding in a race. The filly and I hit the ground hard. I am OK, but I see my horse is not; I hold her until she passes away, right on the track. I am heartbroken, feeling the pain of this beautiful creature, as she dies right before my eyes. I can comprehend the agony, but it is too much for me to handle at times.

After this emotionally draining day, I take myself off mounts for the rest of the week. It is almost the end of the summer, and Saratoga is coming to a close. I stay in New York for the Belmont fall meet. I don't know if I can stay here for the winter—I hate riding in New York in cold weather. When I was younger and just starting out, I had so much adrenaline flowing through my veins it didn't matter to me, but now winter doesn't inspire me to stay. I tell Drew about my plans, and ask him if he would like to follow me to the West Coast, but he says he cannot relocate now with a new family.

Before I venture off to California, I have to ride a horse in the Woodbine Mile in Toronto, Canada. I really don't want to get on a plane and be by myself, but Drew drives me to the airport and persuades me to go. I win the Woodbine Mile on a horse named Geri. It is hell making the weight to ride. I sit in the hotbox, sweating profusely for six hours, wolfing down laxatives and diuretics.

Chapter 81

Serena

My pilgrimage to Israel is upon me, and I will taste the deliciousness of honey and milk. I converted to Judaism a few months back, and I'm still going to temple every Saturday morning. I feel very close to my own immortal being, and the Divine. I'm very excited about being in the biblical land, and will be going on a tour with all Jewish-born people. I had booked another tour a few months ago that was only for the physically fit, but it was cancelled, as not enough people were committed.

I am aware of my soul, and sense I am connected to the Divine. I still have a lot of family issues that I need to resolve. For me, understanding my higher nature when my lower self is in disarray is not fully embracing a serene existence. Before I make my religious journey to the Holy Land, my mother wakes me from a deep sleep in the middle of the night. She calls me on the phone, frantically upset and screaming, "Where is she? Where is Momma?"

I call 911 so the police will be at my mother's house when I arrive, then get into my car and start to speed, as I am in a state of panic.

As I am making the fifteen-minute drive to my mother's house, a police officer comes up behind me, trying to make me pull over. I do not stop, since all I can think about is getting to my mother. As I pull up to my mother's house, I get out of the car and scream at the police officers already at my mother's house, "Tell the cop behind me I am going to see my mother!" I enter my mother's house, and my mother is hysterically crying, still asking, "Where is she?"

She just had a very vivid dream, in which she could not find her mother but was coherent enough to call me in the middle of it all. Here is the cycle of dysfunction: my mother never provided for my needs, and my mother's mother never provided for her needs. I am in the midst of my family trauma, generations of mothers expecting their daughters to provide for them. There is a very important saying: "And the cycle goes on." Only when one of the generations becomes conscious of the situation will it finally change. I feel it is not about blaming someone else. I know it is about becoming aware of the dysfunction, thereby breaking the cycle.

Chapter 82

Serena

The land flowing with milk and honey is waiting for me to embrace its sweetness. I meet my tour group at Newark Airport in New Jersey, and we board our plane, arriving in Jerusalem twelve hours later. I feel amazing, as I step on the soil of this ancient, religious country. At the airport we meet our tour guide, an American Jew who now lives in Israel. He takes us in his minivan to our hotel. We check in and I am tired, so I go to my room and take a nap.

It is Friday, around five o'clock in the afternoon, and we are heading to Mount Scopus. The mountain has a view of the whole city of Jerusalem. I am taking in the beauty of this extraordinary metropolis as we say a prayer in Hebrew, and bless our stay in the Holy Land.

As I move closer to the old town walls, I see the awe-inspiring area of Jerusalem. I witness the Dome of the Rock; this historic mosque is the sacred spot where over two thousand years ago Abraham, the Father of Judaism, almost sacrificed his son Isaac to God. From this same sanctified place, the Prophet Mohammad ascended to heaven. Just a few feet away I see the Wailing Wall, the last remnants of the Temple of Solomon. We stop at the revered wall and welcome in the Sabbath, as I put my prayers between the stones.

All of us say a devout petition to the Divine, and then head back to our hotel for Shabbat dinner. I feel a deep connection to this city. I love the fact that the majority of the people are observing this holy day. It makes me feel very special to be a part of the oneness of this place. As we enter the treasured, old town walls again, I walk the Via Della Rosa, the path Jesus took on his way to be crucified. We then enter the Church of the Holy

Sepulcher, said to be the actual spot where Jesus was crucified and buried.

I feel the three great religions that envelop this city—Judaism, Christianity, and Islam—ideally should be embraced as if they are one. If only we could let go of our personalities, we could see they are three inspired stories given to us as a tool, and we could learn to open up to the true nature of the universe and ourselves.

The sun is warm as the next day arrives, and I leave my group to meet up with an organization I belong to in New York. The Kabbalah Center has a hub here in Jerusalem, so I jump into a taxi and drive about an hour and a half north of the city to an area near the Sea of Galilee. I meet the kabbalah group at a certain point, and board their bus. I am very impressed with the taxi driver, who, seeing I am about to pay him, tells me, "You don't have to pay now—I will come and pick you up." I thank him.

Israel is celebrating a holiday, equivalent to St. Valentine's Day. The people from the Kabbalah Center and I make a spiritual journey to an ancient rabbi's tomb to pray. I've heard it said that the energies from his resting place can connect a person to a soul mate within the year. I meet my taxi driver hours later, in the same spot where he dropped me off. He drives me back to Jerusalem. I pay him for the roundtrip ride, and I walk into my hotel around nine in the evening.

As soon as I hit my pillow, I fall asleep. I only have a few hours for a quiet spell, as our tour leader is waking us up at four in the morning to head south to the desolate Judean Desert. King Herod of ancient Judah built his luxurious palace on top of a mountain in 37 BC. Masada, as it is called, overlooks the Dead Sea. This peak is fourteen hundred feet at the summit, so climbing it on foot is an excellent aerobic workout. Our precious gem, the sun, is rising, a truly magical experience. I am on top of this impressive peak, and I'm just taking in the beauty all around me. I can see the Dead Sea in the distance, and right below are the remnants of Roman camps.

After the destruction of the second temple around 70 BC, a group of Jews flee to the top of this mountain. A small number of Jewish people escape the Romans, and commit suicide instead of surrendering to their enemy. All of us descend via cable car. We get into our minibus and trek deeper into the desert, and then stop for lunch—I eat a delicious falafel sandwich. Now we are driving to the resort on the Dead Sea. We change into our bathing suits, and submerge ourselves in the natural mud baths.

An ancient legend says Cleopatra traveled here from Egypt to soak up the minerals of the Dead Sea. I'm covered from neck to toe in this earthy matter, and I arise from the bottom of the pond looking like a creature from the black lagoon. The sun is beating down on me as my feet step onto the burning hot sand. I need to slide a few feet to the water. I am walking right into the lowest point on earth as I step into the Dead Sea. The water is very salty and stingy. Once you are in this body of water, you don't swim—you float! It is a surreal experience, resting in this water in the middle of the desert.

I change out of my bathing suit, and into street clothes. We are heading back to our hotel. Our itinerary says that after the Dead Sea, we will stop at Qumran. The people in my group are too tired to encounter this site, so I have to coax my tour guide to park and let us explore. We arrive in Qumran and just three of us—myself, the tour leader and one guy from the group—get out of the bus. The sun is glaring down, making me terribly hot, but it is fascinating to be standing here, looking out onto the caves where the Dead Sea scrolls were found.

We get back onto the bus and it seems that the people who stayed behind (which is most of them) are annoyed at me. I have so much passion within that I want to see all these awe-inspiring sites, while all they want to do is sit by the pool. That is what we do when we get back to the hotel: we sit by the swimming pool. We eat dinner in Jerusalem, and everyone is tired, so we go to sleep early. The next day we are going to a kibbutz near the Sea of Galilee. In the minibus, we drive an hour and a half north to the kibbutz, a community that makes women's hair-removal products. I don't particularly like staying on this commune. The accommodations are fine, but the place where we eat is a cafeteria—the food is OK, but I like ambiance when I eat.

Another hot sunny day is upon us as we go to visit the mystical town of Safed, the center of the kabbalah in the sixteenth century. This divinely-inspired city is surrounded by mountains covered in pine trees. The breathtaking views encircling this area are otherworldly. I break away from my group and my tour guide, and I climb about one hundred steps to a cemetery in the hills of this enigmatic place. A prominent rabbi of the kabbalah is buried here. When I approach his revered grave, I am confronted with an enormous amount of energy radiating from this tomb.

After my amazing experience, the tour guide and I meet up with the group, as they were shopping in town. All of us head toward a wine-tasting shop, and I sip some delicious wine from the Galilee area. After getting a little tipsy, we enter a temple and pray. We are going back to the kibbutz for dinner. "How lovely," I say sardonically.

As we are driving I see the Sea of Galilee. I ask the tour guide if we can stop to take a picture, but he refuses. He says to me, "I like your passion, but we just can't stop."

I say, "OK," but I am not happy with the decision. As I turn my head to the left I see the Sea of Galilee passing me. Everyone is tired except me, but all of us eat and then go to sleep. The next day is a free day, and all we do is lie around by the pool. It is time for dinner and we go to a restaurant in Tiberius.

Tiberius lies on the western shore of the Sea of Galilee. It is named after the Roman Emperor Tiberius. It is said that Jesus performed miracles here. It is dark, and all of us, including my tour guide, are standing on a street deciding where to go. For some reason, I have to use the ladies' room. All week I have been waiting for everyone in the group to use the bathroom, but now I have to go and tell the tour guide I am going into the hotel across the street to use the bathroom. He says, "OK, we'll wait." I come out of the hotel maybe five to seven minutes later. I cross the street and start to panic, as my clan is nowhere in sight. I am scared out of my wits, as I can't pronounce the name of the kibbutz, because it's in Hebrew. So I can't take a taxi, and I don't know what I am going to do. I am getting very nervous, stranded on the streets of Tiberius.

About ten minutes later, I see my tour guide walking towards me. I start screaming at him, "I waited all week for everyone else: why couldn't you wait for me?"

He doesn't say anything, and walks me to the restaurant to meet the group. I am so full of fear and anger at the same time that my needs are not being met. I will attract the same scenario into my life over and over until I make the connection. My mother emotionally abandoned me the day I was conceived. She never wanted me, and never made me feel part of the family. Someday I will have to make this emotional connection to discover why this scenario of not belonging keeps attracting me. I will eventually have to understand that I do matter, and deserve to be treated with respect.

That day is not today, and I feel ashamed that I am not included in this group of people. I leave Tiberius with a bad taste in my mouth. We head towards the hotel, and I fall right to sleep. The next day the sun is shining, and we spend the whole day on the bus driving to Tel Aviv.

Tel Aviv is the second largest city in Israel. The city has a secular feel, as opposed to Jerusalem. We check into our hotel, which overlooks the Mediterranean Sea. We have two days left in Israel, and our time is spent lying on the beach. My trip to this ancient religious land is about to end.

A few people from the tour are going to Eliat near the Red Sea, but the majority of us are on our way home. I just traveled to an exotic country, and I don't feel good about myself. I felt left out of my group, and I didn't make any real connections. Feeling like I don't belong is a major obstacle in my life that I need to overcome. It has brought negativity at school, and in my life in general. I have tasted being at one with my immortal soul, but I still have a long way to go until I become whole, where my personality and soul are one and the same.

Chapter 83

Chris

I hear a whisper from within: *go west, young man.* I return to the state of California.

I just can't do it anymore. I don't have it in me to reduce my weight. I don't have the eye of the tiger. I've lost the passion. Emotionally, I am so low. I am not getting the mounts I used to. Now the California Racing Board wants me to take a drug test, but I refuse to take it because I know I will not pass. I tell the racing executives I'm going to take some time off.

Knowing I might not ever ride again. I check myself into a hotel, and spend the next six weeks stoned out of my mind. My agent Ron Anderson comes by and checks on me, and some friends are looking out for me too. Ultimately I am depressed, fat, and alone with my drugs. "I didn't want to go out in public because people would see how big I was and how I failed. I tried every diet there was, knowing that I would probably not be back. I was in solitary confinement, staring at the walls. I was depressed, lower than low, out of it for a month and a half."[lviii] One day Ron comes by, and refuses to leave without me.

He drags me into rehab, and off I go. I am scheduled to do the usual twenty-eight days, but I want to stay longer. It's January 1, 1998. Today is the day that all thoroughbreds in the Northern Hemisphere turn a year older. *I am sitting in the lounge of the rehab center, reading a book entitled Conversations with God.*[lix] *I love this book and feel very connected to its message. The back cover of the book reads: "I have heard the crying of your heart. I have seen the searching of your soul. I know how deeply you have desired the truth."*[lx]

I hear my immortal soul speak to me. I think I have ignored my divine gift within me for a very long time. It is in rehab that I can be vulnerable, and listen to what my higher self is telling me.

I don't want to leave, as I feel at home here in this safe haven. I want to do something for the people here, so I fix a couple of bedrooms, and I give my television set to them. Deep down, I feel I can make a difference here. By the time summer arrives, the staff feels I should be out in the real world. I apply for my jockey license again, but I am very overweight. I leave rehab and move in with Ron, but I can't ride. Ron describes me to other people in a lovely way: "He is very generous and kind. Very warm and great with kids. My granddaughter loves him. Chris just has a way."[lxi]

My dear friend Gary Stevens is getting married for the second time, and asks me to be his best man. A couple of days later I fly to Las Vegas for his wedding. *He knew I was spiritually gifted, and over the years Gary and I have lengthy discussions about our spiritual beliefs. We question whether there is a personal God, or some other Higher Being.*[lxii]

I don't know what to do with my life. Within weeks, I am deeply depressed again. I see that my life as I knew it for the past fifteen years is over. Luckily, money is not a problem, but I don't know what I am going to do with my life. I decide I want to go home to South Carolina.

Chapter 84

Serena

My flight from Israel has just landed in New York. I feel let down. I didn't have the spiritual experience I thought I would have. I had so much passion before I left. I thought I was going to have the time of my life. A person's high expectations can hinder a divine experience. Now I am home wondering where I belong. I am back in a state of depression.

I wasn't identified with my true self in Israel. I have been working on my issues for six years now, but I still have not developed into a healthy, functioning human. The plane went up in the air again but could not sustain the altitude, and came crashing down.

Being in the Holy Land did not produce a state of enlightenment for me. My soul was not at the forefront of this trip. My personality was in total control, and could not unite with my immortal being. It is now the end of September in the year 1997. I look in the newspaper to see if Chris Antley is still riding here in New York. I notice he has left, but I think nothing of this news, and glide on with my life.

In the autumn of 1997 the little girl in me is in a deep depression. I feel isolated and alone, and the frustration I suffer within me is overwhelming at times. Basically, throughout my six years in therapy, it is clear that I have to figure out for myself the origins to my problems.

I feel a therapist is there for you to give you support, and not the answers. I am feeling deep shame that I'm not good enough. I need to bring my shame out in the open and make it a feeling again, so that it will not stay hidden within me for the rest of my life. If the feeling I'm not good enough stays in the dark, I am doomed. I must face it to be rid of it.

I am in this slump of gloom, but what always makes me feel good for the moment is getting away. Marcy and I are talking about taking a journey to Rome, as we would like to ring in the New Year of 1998 in Italy. I can't wait to go and see the famed Coliseum and Forum. We book our flights, and Marcy and I are on our way to have a fabulous Roman holiday!

Chapter 85

Serena

The Alitalia aircraft is up in the troposphere, and Marcy and I are on our way to Rome. We caught the plane by a narrow margin. Marcy left the tickets on top of her microwave oven, and the powerful heat melted the paper. The airline is not going to let us get on the flight, but we call the travel agent, and we are able to receive new tickets. We settle in, and I nod off for five hours; when I wake up, I feel well rested.

Marcy dozes too, but I don't think she has enough rest, because when we land and check into our hotel room, all she wants to do is sleep. I decide to take the ten-minute walk to the Roman Coliseum by myself. When I spot a private tour with a guide explaining the history of the stadium, I hook up with them, and we explore inside the arena. I spend about two hours at the amphitheater, and then I strut back to the hotel. Marcy is just getting up, and I assume she is well rested.

In a couple of hours we are off to a New Year's Eve party. Marcy says to me, "I feel fabulous, and I'm looking forward to the party."

I say, "Great." We put on nice attire, and walk around the block to another hotel. We have some wine and pasta for dinner, and then the restaurant turns into a dance floor. We jiggle all night, into the wee hours of 1998. The next day, we wake up late and explore the city of Rome. The breathtaking sight of the Coliseum is so exciting to me.

We stop at a fast-food concession stand by the Coliseum, where I buy a mouthwatering salami and provolone cheese hero. We stroll down side streets, and wander into the Roman Forum, and there I sit in a meditative state on a stone absorbing my surroundings. I can imagine myself here centuries ago, when Rome ruled the world. Marcy and I like to stroll, so we cross the River

Tiber and enter a medieval neighborhood. We wander in and out of the area for the rest of the day. Then we cross over the river once more, heading back to our hotel. We hit our pillows, and take a restful nap.

Dinnertime is here, and just up the block is a small pizzeria where we eat some pasta, drink some wine and then head back to our hotel. The next day we sign up for a one-day tour at the Vatican Museum. The rain is pounding on us as we wait in line to enter the historic site. We proceed inside the building, and I journey in silence. I approach the awe-inspiring masterpiece of Michelangelo, his exalted creation, the Sistine Chapel.

I look up with reverence, as I witness the presence of a sublime conception. Marcy and I don't say one word to one another until we move toward St. Peter's Basilica. The massive courtyard that envelops St. Peter's is powerful. This is the most grand and priceless cathedral on earth. Even the rain doesn't deter me from absorbing the magnificence of this little city within a big city.

After experiencing something this profound, we have to get something to eat and a glass of wine to celebrate. As we are eating, Marcy and I enter into a heated argument. She doesn't like how the conversation is going, and says to me, "I'm not going with you to meet our friend tonight."

I am livid. "What do you mean you are not coming with me?" I feel abandoned, and she wants to make a point. I start to withdraw, and say to her, "Just leave me alone for a while." We walk quickly to our hotel, and she keeps talking, but I just want to get over the feeling of being abandoned.

When we get to our hotel room, I shut the door with force, and Marcy wants to leave Italy. She is packing up her belongings, and heading out the door. I say, "What are you doing?"

She replies, "I'm leaving."

I say, "Don't go." We talk it out, but there is a heavy feeling of negativity in the air. She comes with me, and we meet Mel (a friend from our Europe trip) at a restaurant in the center of Rome. Marcy and I eventually make up, but there is tension between us for the rest of the week.

A soft chill is in the air the next day as we are strolling around Rome. I hear the sound of a waterfall. I look to my right, and there it is: the Trevi Fountain. A huge statue of the god Neptune overlooks his horses, and a flow of water cascades over the marble stone. The dramatic work of art creates an inspiring ambiance around the water brought in by the city's aqueducts. I throw three coins in the fountain, and make a wish to meet a soul mate. After marveling at the water and stone creation, we follow our hearts and enter Piazza Navona. From a distance I see the Fountain of the Four Rivers.

Intuitively Marcy and I trace the course of water that rushes from the Trevi Fountain and flows through the Fountain of the Four Rivers: the Nile of Africa, the Danube of Europe, the Ganges of Asia, and the Rio de la Plata of the Americas. The seventeenth-century Italian Baroque sculptor Gian Lorenzo Bernini honored all these in his design.

Piazza Navona is filled with colorful balloons and concession stands gearing up for the Festival of the Epiphany in a couple of days. We enter a restaurant and sit at one of the outside tables, as we sip a cappuccino. We are enjoying watching the people pass us by.

I am talking to Marcy, asking her if she wants to go to Pompeii tomorrow on a one-day tour. We will have to get up early and make the bus for the three-hour trip to the ancient ruins. Marcy is not too happy with the idea. She doesn't want to spend the one hundred dollars for the adventure. I tell her to think about it, but soon realize she doesn't want to go.

Later that day, as we are having dinner, I ask her again if she wants to go to Pompeii. She says, "No, I don't want to go."

I say to her, "It's not fair to go without you. I will not go." Yet I am annoyed. Here we are in Rome, with a chance to see an awesome site. I make my decision not to go.

We wake up late the next day, and both of us do our own thing. I skip to the Coliseum again, and enter the train station at the arena. I have my guidebook with me, and follow the directions for a thirty-minute train ride to Ostia Antica.

Ostia Antica is ancient Rome's port city. Ancient docks, warehouses, and apartment buildings envelop the city. The museum is closed today, but the weather is warm, so I walk around the town. After about an hour and a half, I hop on the train, and back to Rome I go. I get off at my stop, and proceed to the hotel. I feel so elated that I was able to explore and go out on my own. Marcy is in the room reading. I ask her, "How was your day?"

She says, "It was OK."

About an hour later we strut along the Via Veneto (the Rodeo Drive of Rome). The Italian designer Gucci inspires us to step into the store, and I purchase a gorgeous belt. Marcy doesn't like anything from Gucci, so we head towards Fendi. The Italian brand stirs Marcy to buy a Fendi pocketbook, and I buy a pair of boots that are on sale. After our shopping spree, we have dinner; I order veal piccata; Marcy has fish, and we share a bottle of wine.

We take our last saunter around town as we celebrate the Epiphany at the Piazza Navona. It is a warm night and a delight to be strolling and celebrating the eve of this holiday with the Romans. When in Rome, do as the Romans do! Tomorrow is the celebration of the three Wise Men who saw the shining star in the east. They brought divine gifts to the Messiah. I feel at one with the whole concept of celebrating in the piazza. It is a great experience being here for the Epiphany. Growing up, my mother always called this holiday Little Christmas. I now see it is a very important holiday in Italy. In the back of my mind I think about Chris, knowing January the sixth is his birthday.

Marcy and I wake up fairly early on the sixth, and we're off to the airport to board a flight back to New York. I had a growing experience with Marcy; would I say it was fantastic? No. But personal growth is not easy, and I did experience Italy. Between traveling our beautiful world and expanding my mind, this trip was worth my time and money.

Chapter 86

Chris

I am fat, depressed, and back home in rural South Carolina.

It's over, my life as I know it…is finished. I'm so overweight my eyes have lost their shine, and I'm here where I started. Don't get me wrong. It's great seeing my family. But I am so emotionally unstable, and I have failed. I am living with my father and step-mom Annie, and I just sleep, get up, and watch television. I don't have a purpose, and I am so low, I can't function.

My father collected most of my racing memorabilia, and I can't stand looking at what I used to be. It makes me sad, frustrated, and angry. My father says, "Chris, you have enough money—do something else."[lxiii] I don't feel that is the right move for me. I am so out of place, and I don't have a direction. Weeks go by, and I am comatose: I just don't have any life in me, and eat my way through my deep despair. I am 147 pounds, wearing a big T-shirt. I'm sitting by my computer when I realize I have a natural aptitude for the stock market.

I research companies, and I can see which ones are profitable, so I become a day trader, and give my picks to my followers with my *Ant Man Report*.[lxiv] Yet, I feel my passion for the stock market is just a hobby. I was a top race rider once, and deep down I know that is where I should be, on the racetrack. I don't have a clue how to get back there.

One day as I am gazing at the television set, I start to watch a horse race. I later tell a reporter what I felt while I watched: "I really felt low. I used to do that, I feel like I cheated myself through my whole career."[lxv] I also later remember: "It brought me to a cold reality that it was the one thing I loved."[lxvi]

Tears well up in my eyes, but something rattles inside of me and I know what I want. I am going to make a comeback—I am going to ride racehorses again! The next day the sun is sparkling, as I have seen the light! I start talking with a psychotherapist, and invest in some good sneakers. I am going to cut carbohydrates from my diet, and begin my weight reduction. *I feel I'm connecting with my immortal essence. Afterwards, I describe the change to a writer: "I had dug deep into the depths of my soul and faced down some monsters."*[lxvii] My dark nights are over. I can feel it. I have a purpose: my mission is to get this weight off, and ride again. *I'm drawing on the strength of my inner depths*!

Chapter 87

Serena

Rome is a thought away, as I am home and back in the grind again. Day in and day out, I hop in my car and drive to each and every one of my clients. I know I am a good personal trainer, as I love to motivate people. I jog about two miles with five out of my thirty people about two to three times a week. I even speak with them about my passion for the stock market as I am invested in high quality companies. I also have them lift weights, and then I stretch their bodies.

One day in between customers I'm browsing in a bookstore, and I spot a book that looks interesting to me. *Twin Souls: A Guide to Finding Your True Spiritual Partner.* The back cover reads: "You can know that you are indissolubly linked with another. Your meeting is destined."[lxviii] I go home and I start to read this treasured work. Right away, I am blown away by the material. The message throughout the pages resonates deep within my being.

The publication informs me about that the soul is directed to find its other half. On and off for the past four years, meditation has been a part of my life. Now in my focused state, I start to concentrate on connecting with a close soul.

A few weeks go by, and one night when my head hits the pillow, Chris Antley appears in my dreams. I wake up, and think nothing of this sleeping vision. I am not involved with horse racing anymore, so I really don't pay attention.

≈

Chapter 88

Chris

Feeling motivated, I am connecting with my divine, internal self.

Something inside of me has taken control. I am so focused on returning to my soul's passion. I can feel my immortal being embracing me, and saying, "Come on Chris, you can do it."

I feel inspired by God, and I run up to twenty-five miles a day.[lxix] I get the name Forrest Gump from all the people in Columbia, South Carolina, from the gas station to the grocery store to the bookstore and all the shops I run past. I become a regular, passing member of town. I knew I was going to get there. Where there's a will, there's a way.[lxx]

I feel like superman: I have a purpose and I am going to ride racehorses, yes! I think to myself, it would be great to ride in the Kentucky Derby again. Then I think I am taking this too far. I need to think about today, not tomorrow.

As my alarm clock jolts me out of bed at the break of dawn, I put on my sweatshirt and pants. I tie my super sneakers, grab an apple, and I'm out the door. There is a chill in the air, but I don't mind. I absorb the atmosphere. I am jogging on the country roads. I am alone, but I'm not lonely; I feel at one with the universe. I'm connecting with the Divine as my deep inner essence is sparkling with delight. My determination to get back in the saddle is unwavering.

The sun is high in the sky as I have been running for hours, and I am exhausted. I need to rest, so I stop at the Piggly Wiggly for some water. The sweat is dripping off my body like a waterfall, but I continue for another four hours of jogging. I want to stop: my muscles are not getting the oxygen they need and I'm fatiguing, but I did it—now I'm back at my father's, and I can feel I'm almost at my goal weight.

On days when the weather is not suitable for running outside, I go to the gym and work out, and *I can sometimes see myself from the top of the room.*[lxxi] I am wonderstruck. My divine gift within is rising beyond time and space. Some people call this having an out-of-body experience. *A number of theologians see out-of-body occurrences as profoundly spiritual. They say it is a verification of our immortality.*

Chapter 89

Serena

Almost every night I enter a deep meditative state, connecting my immortal being with another. When I go to sleep, I see Chris Antley and me in my night visions playing ping-pong, and I win. I wake up, and ignore what I just dreamt. It makes no sense to me that I would be dreaming about Chris. I feel my life with racehorses was over a long time ago.

I don't know why my past is appearing in the present. So I continue with my life as I keep meditating. After a couple of months, I wake up in the middle of the night from these sleeping visions, calling Chris's name. I keep asking why I am dreaming about him, but I do not receive an answer. I'm on a weekend getaway in Atlantic City in August 1998. I just happen to pass the horse racing section of the casino.

I stop to see if Chris is riding in California, and notice I don't see his name on any horse. I don't know why I even check to see if he is riding. I don't have an interest in horse racing anymore. I don't realize Chris is not on my conscious mind, but he is deeply embedded in my unconscious.

A month goes by, and I have a vivid dream that I am riding horses in the country. I am with two gentlemen, and one is my lover who tells me he can see heaven in my eyes. The other man is my brother. The three of us have a love for horses. At this point I do not know the meaning of this profound dream.

≈

Chapter 90

Chris

I am almost within range of my riding weight.

I have been working out hard, and controlling my diet. I'm just about at my goal, but my knee starts to radiate pain throughout my whole body. I can't walk, and unfortunately I have to be on the sidelines. I can't afford to take weeks off now, not now, but I don't have a choice: the pain is unbearable. Within a couple of weeks, however, I am up and training again. The conviction I feel deep inside me is not going to give up. I know deep down I must ride racehorses once more. I can't stay in South Carolina and hide for the rest of my life.

I want to achieve something with people. I want to help them learn something rewarding.[lxxii] *I want to send a message about real life, and about what people really have inside of them—the insecurities people really have, the hidden part, behind the scenes of how people really feel, the pain and suffering a lot go through, who can't tell their story.*[lxxiii]

The only way I know how to bring my message to people is for me to be within riding weight. From there, I can work my way to the top of the sport of horse racing again. Then, I can be the voice for those who don't have a platform.

Now I'm down to 118 pounds. Happy and content, I call up Ron, "I will be ready to ride in a few weeks." My agent is galvanized, and I tell him, "I'm coming to California in January."

He says, "Great! You can stay at my house with me and my family."

≈

Chapter 91

Serena

As I am meditating consistently, I keep having dreams of Chris. One night I wake up from a vision calling his name. I think, *is he all right? Is he alive?* I speculate for a moment that he has gone to the spirit world. I don't have any idea why he would come into my dreams, even if his soul were on the other side. I think, *if he has died, what a waste of two gorgeous eyes.*

Morning arrives. I open my eyes, and ask myself how I am going to find out if he is all right. I remember that I have a client who has a gift shop at the racetrack. I ask her, "Is Chris Antley still riding?"

She says, "Yes, he is." He is all right, so I proceed with life. As time goes on, I still have sleeping visions about Chris. When I wake up, I still keep wondering why I am dreaming about him.

I joke to myself, *Chris is my soul mate, and from his addictions he became spiritual.* I don't consciously realize that what I am saying has a lot of validity to it. I do not comprehend what transpired in the past between us was so deep and profound. I do not understand that years ago Chris was much more spiritually aware than I was. I am meditating on a regular basis, and listening to my immortal being. Then I see an ad in a magazine: *Come to Greece and have conversations with God.*

≈

Chapter 92

Serena

I'm on my way to the legendary country of Greece. I'm up in the sky in man's greatest invention—the airplane. It's awesome that the land of the gods and goddesses awaits me. I am traveling alone again, and I will be meeting my tour in Athens. I feel great I am going to have a conversation with God on the same ground Plato wandered. Plato is an important teacher of mine; he understood the knowledge of our immortal soul twenty-five hundred years ago.

One sultry night in ancient Greece, Socrates and five other philosophers join together, and the *Symposium* is created. Plato, a student of Socrates, writes down the dialogue in which these enormous thinkers are engaged. This great literary work about love has survived the ages. These amazing men of thought gave us wisdom about two types of love: common love and celestial love.

To understand common love is very simple: it is found in our everyday relationships. Celestial love is an extraordinary bond, the aim of which is to connect our gift from the Divine with another person. So here I am at Athens airport, boarding a flight to the island of Crete.

One night, many moons ago, thunder rumbles in the sky, and from a dark cave on Crete, Zeus comes into being. Zeus makes the island flourish and develop into an advanced civilization. He situated the island far south in the Aegean Sea. While we are still at the airport waiting for our bus, I meet some people from my tour. The van comes and takes us to our home for the week: a five-star resort on this mythical island.

Poseidon, the god of the seas, creates the oceans of the earth. The Tritons blow their breath into their shells, making the body of water swell and recede. Poseidon takes advantage of this momentum, so that his sea-chariot, drawn by his horses, travels the vast oceans with lightning speed. The magnificent sea that Poseidon designed surrounds the island of Crete. We enter our beachfront complex, and are greeted with drinks.

The sun is shining, and it's a comfortable, warm spring day. The hotel staff picks me up in a golf cart, and we drive to my villa. I look out my window, and I am happily surprised by the private pool. I have a few hours before the whole group gets together for introductions. I take an hour-long nap, and before I know it, it's time to meet the crowd. The tour leader makes a speech, welcoming us to this fabled island. We are going to encounter the author of the book, *Conversations with God.*

I thought I was going to have a profound talk with God. I didn't realize it had anything to do with the book. I think this should be very interesting anyway. I turn my head and see a woman whom I met on my first visit to Egypt. "Hi Kimberly," I say. "Do you remember me?"

She says, "Yes." Kimberly had died for an hour and a half, and lived to tell about her experience. She is one of the presenters telling her story here on Crete. Kimberly and I hang out, until she has to leave and mingle.

It is time for dinner, and all one hundred of us gather in the dining room. I spot a table with an open seat and ask, "Is anyone sitting here?"

"No," one woman says, and we start to talk, and have remained dear friends ever since. Her name is Lenore, a petite, pretty woman with red hair. She lives on Staten Island, New York, and is here because she loves the book, *Conversations With God.* After dinner, I am tired from my long day of travel, and head to bed.

Morning wakes me with the sound of birds on a tree outside by the sparkling pool. I head over to the main dining room for breakfast, and say good morning to Lenore. I have Greek yogurt and honey, coffee, and juice. After we eat, we meet our group in the lobby.

Crete's history is centered on the Minoans, the people of an ancient civilization. We are on our way by bus to Knossos, the ceremonial and political center of the Minoan civilization. The Minoans lived around the same time as the ancient Egyptians. Since their architecture is very similar, historians don't know who influenced whom. As I am rambling around this historic site, I can't help but think about King Minos…

King Minos is a son of Zeus, and ruler of ancient Crete. His treasured palace is Knossos. King Minos's wife and Poseidon decide to give the king a gift to inspire him to ascend the Cretan throne. They choose to present him with a white bull, a sign of good luck. They intend for the bull to be sacrificed to the gods, but Minos so admires the bull that he decides to keep it. As punishment, the gods cause Minos's wife to fall in love with the bull. The queen mates with the animal, and gives birth to the Minotaur, a hideous half-bull, half-human monster. The Minotaur demands that he be fed fourteen Athenian youth every year—seven boys and seven girls. A man named Theseus wants to free Athens from this horrible fate, so he travels to Crete and enters the labyrinth where the creature lives. Theseus kills the Minotaur, and finds his way out of the complex, symbolizing King Minos's loss of the Cretan throne.

We finish our beautiful visit to this ancient site, and head to the gift shop. I buy a few items, including a simple Greco-Roman-style photo frame. I get back on the bus and a few of us, Lenore included, spend some time exploring the small town near our hotel. It is sunny and warm, and I decide to go back to the hotel after lunch in town. I take advantage of my private pool, and I'm absorbing the sun's rays on my body. I stay by the pool the rest of the day.

I make my way to dinner, and afterward we hear a lecture by the author of *Conversations with God*. The writer is in his late fifties, and looks like he comes from the Midwest. What he says does make a lot of sense, and I take what I feel resonates for me.

When the lecture is over, Lenore and I meet some people at the indoor pool. The space is transformed into a dance floor. Spotlights are used to enhance the spectacular ambiance of the darkened room. I dance until the wee hours of the morning.

That night Morpheus, the god of dreams, comes into my sleep as I see a vision of the nineteenth-century French academic artist William Bouguereau's *Aphrodite*. I meet the goddess of love as she is explained in Lucius Apuleius's *The Golden Ass*. Love is forming out of a shell in the middle of the sea just off the island of Cyprus. Gods and goddesses of the ocean are welcoming Aphrodite onto the earth.

Poseidon's tritons are blowing charismatic music into the air, creating a sound the world will know as love.

Aphrodite is unashamed of her body. She exudes sensuality, and is welcomed by angels who want to show her and the world that true love is within our reach. Venus (her Roman name) is the key that unlocks the door to immortal love. She leads us to reach for the ultimate nonattachment to another person.

I wake up from my dream, and I am wowed by what a night vision that was. I know I need to purchase a statue of the goddess Aphrodite before I leave this country. We spend the next couple of days on Crete soaking up the sun and listening to lectures.

Our time on Crete ends, and now we are waiting outside the resort for our bus ride to the airport. Overhead we see NATO planes, fighting in the Kosovo war. We make it to the airport in one piece, and fly to Athens.

Athens is famous for the Acropolis, an exalted city constructed on a sacred rock. High on the top of this hill is the seat from which the ancient Greeks ruled their country, complete with temples and theatres. I am standing at sea level, looking at the Acropolis, and I am in awe of the classic beauty of the Greek architecture. The Parthenon is the symbol of ancient Greece, where the origins of democracy flourished. Its design influences almost the entire Western world.

We only stay in Athens overnight, and I am disappointed we don't have more time in this very special city. Half of the group is going back to the States, including Lenore. I am going with the other half, which will be leaving for the island of Santorini in a few hours.

A forty-five-minute plane ride from Athens brings us to the picturesque, volcanic island of Santorini. When we check into our hotel, it is late at night, so a few of us head to a restaurant for a late-night snack. I eat a small Greek salad, and drink some wine. After Dionysus, the Greek god of winemaking, coaxes me to enjoy two glasses, my body feels tired, so I head to my room and sleep like a baby.

My eyes open to the brightness of the sun shining through the window. I look out and the stunning view of the deep blue water of the Aegean is breathtaking. This hotel is built into the majestic cliffs of this island. I sit and meditate on the terrace for a while, absorbing the beauty.

I decide to order room service for breakfast, instead of eating in the dining room. I just can't help myself: I want to continue experiencing the view. I hear a knock at the door, and my Greek yogurt and honey, coffee, and juice have arrived. I'm sitting outside, savoring the delicious meal and the exotic scenery. *OK, come back to this world*, I say to myself. It's time to go down to the lobby and meet my group, as we plan to visit Akrotiri.

Thirty-six hundred years ago, the city of Akrotiri was destroyed in one of the largest volcanic eruptions known to man. As soon as I step on the ground of this archeological site, I feel an immediate connection. I witness rows and rows of pottery that survived the ages. Historians consider Akrotiri one possible location for the legendary lost city of Atlantis. Plato talks about Atlantis in his work *Critias*. The awesome philosopher describes the utopian society as having "…many temples for different gods, and many gardens and areas for exercise, some for men and some for horses. On the middle of the larger island in particular there was a special course for horse racing."[lxxiv]

After our walk back in time, we have lunch in town looking out over the sparkling waters of the Aegean. We spend the rest of the day on the beach soaking up the sun. There are about thirty of us who are left from the original one hundred. I am hanging out with Trudy, an older woman, and Paul, a middle-aged man.

At dusk we eat at a nice restaurant overlooking the enchanted landscape. I order fish and Greek wine, and it is delicious. About fifteen of us, including Trudy and Paul, are feeling good as we enter a bar. There is a band playing music in the corner. I order a chocolate martini and after a couple of hours the locals are dancing on top of the bar. Everyone is having a great time. Trudy leaves early, and I stay a while longer. I fall asleep thinking about the turquoise-blue waters of the sea, and the feathery clouds of the sky.

In the depth of my sleep I see Morpheus again and now he shows me William Bouguereau's *Eros and Psyche in Heaven*. On a fluffy cloud, young Eros, the true spiritual connection that binds soul mates together, gives Psyche, who represents our soul, a kiss. This painted vision suggests the soul's home is in heaven. We first meet our spiritual mates in our eternal residence. At the deepest level, our identity is imprinted on each other forever.

I wake up the next morning to the gorgeous sun gleaming through my window. I rush downstairs to see Trudy, and we head into the dining room for breakfast. I have my usual Greek yogurt and honey. I say to Trudy, “I found out we are not going to spend any more time in Athens.”

“Yes, our few hours in Athens a couple of days ago was all the time allotted on this tour,” she replies. Then Trudy asks me, “How do you feel about leaving Santorini early? We could go to Athens, and meet up with our tour at Delphi.”

I say, “OK let’s do it,” as I want to see more of Athens.

I call up the airline to see if we can change our flight. The lady on the phone says, “Not a problem.” Trudy and I take a taxi to the Santorini airport, and wait for our flight.

As we are waiting in the airport, I go into one of the gift shops and spot a book called *The Love Life of the Ancient Greeks*. I start to look through the written work and I am stunned: the book talks about the oldest god in Greek mythology, Eros. I purchase the book immediately. I start to absorb all the past knowledge that the Greeks had about a charismatic connection of the soul. As I am leaving the island of Santorini and heading towards Athens, I am engulfed by the profound wisdom I’m reading. Anybody who is searching for Eros has a very high aim.

The goal of Eros is for people to connect with each other at the deepest immortal level. The ancients say having sexual pleasure with another is not Eros. We can have sexual intercourse with or without this profound connection.

We land in Athens, and Trudy and I take a taxi to our hotel. We are spending a night, and meeting our tour in Delphi tomorrow. We put our luggage in our room and proceed to the Temple of Zeus. It has been said the Temple of Zeus rivaled the Pyramids of Giza in Egypt in ancient times.

Unfortunately, the Temple of Zeus is not as well preserved as the pyramids are today. In its heyday, the building was massive, and housed the statue of Zeus, one of the seven ancient wonders of the world. Today Zeus is gone, and all that is left of the building are about a dozen worn columns. Trudy and I are happy we are able to experience the ruins of this remarkable site.

It is such a beautiful, sunny, and warm day, and we dawdle along to the Plaka. The Plaka is a little village within the big city.

There are shops and restaurants galore in this part of town. We stop at a restaurant, and order a Greek salad to eat at one of their outside tables.

As we are walking to the restaurant, I see my Aphrodite in a store window. After lunch Trudy and I enter the store, and I inquire about the statue. I fall in love with this piece of alabaster sculpted into the *Venus de Milo*. The gorgeous piece of stone is three feet high and nine inches in width, so I have to have it shipped to the United States. I am elated I found my goddess of love.

Now that our bellies are full and our shopping spree over, we stroll around the city of Athens for a while. Trudy and I just happen to stumble on the site where Athena, the goddess of wisdom, planted olive trees. It just so happens that this is where Plato decided to build his school. Here we are at the site where the Italian Renaissance artist Raphael was inspired to paint *The School of Athens*, and where in ancient times men would come and learn philosophy, mathematics, and work out their bodies in the gymnasium. About a twenty-minute walk from the Academy is the Athens Museum.

We venture in and I am astonished at the high level of skill in figure representation on the pottery and sculpture. I ask Trudy, "How come we can't create such magnificence in today's world?"

She answers, "Today we can travel to see the magnificence."

I acknowledge, "That makes a lot of sense."

I turn my head, and I view a bronze horse that is in full gallop, as if he is running in a race. His rider is riding bareback with his left arm up, pointing his index finger to the sky as if he has won the race. I think of my past as soon as I see this galloping horse and rider. This true-to-life sculpture was found in the 1970s after two thousand years under the sea.

By now it's late in the afternoon, and we decide to head to our hotel. We rest and have an early dinner, then hit our pillows relatively early, and Hypnos, the god of sleep, brings us rest.

In the morning, the front desk gives me a wakeup call. Then Trudy and I get dressed and have breakfast at the hotel. We have hired a taxi for the one-hundred-mile trip northwest from

Athens to the majestic mountain region and spiritual city of Delphi.

As the legend goes, Zeus released two eagles: one from the west and the other from the east. Both eagles met at Delphi at the same time. From then on Delphi was considered the center of the world in ancient times. Trudy and I have arrived at the navel of the earth. Our group is already at the hotel, and we greet everyone. People from our tour want to know what we did in Athens, and we tell them about our journey. They agree it sounds like we had an interesting time.

The tour leader announces, "We are going to explore Delphi in an hour." I check into my hotel room and freshen up and meet Trudy downstairs in the hotel for lunch. We have a Greek salad and water while we read about the mythology of Delphi.

Apollo, the god of prophecy, art, and music, is the son of Zeus. Apollo fought a python, an earth creature who held dominion over Delphi. The python and Apollo fought from morning until dusk. Apollo triumphed, and Delphi became his domain. At this site of the battle, the Temple of Apollo was erected.

In the inner depths of the temple, the python's mother created an enigmatic mist. A virgin priestess inhaled the vapors, and was seduced by the prophetic voices of Apollo. Petitioners who wanted to know about their future had to perform a sacrifice and pay a fee. Then they would be admitted to see the priestess.

The Oracle at Delphi became world-renowned. On the outer stones of the temple are carved guidelines for how to live a good life. Written on these walls is the foundation for a great society. In order for the general public to grow and flourish, not only economically but also morally, people must have self-awareness. The injunctions, "Know thyself" and "Nothing in excess," are requirements for an advanced civilization.

I go off on my own and start walking the country road, views of majestic mountains in front of me. The Castilian Springs are to my left. If I were one of the visitors here two thousand years ago, waiting to be admitted into the hidden chamber, I would come to the springs. I would wash myself before entering the holy room, and I would be in reverence of the high priestess.

I am here in last months of the twentieth century, so I fill a bottle with the sacred water and continue exploring the area. I stumble onto the Temple of Athena. The circular stones of this temple are the remnants of Doric-style columns. Only three restored columns are still standing. The limestone mountains in the background create an opulent view. Sitting down on one of the outer stones, I begin to meditate.

I begin to go in a trance as I see the elevation of the earth's surface. I begin to have visions of William Bouguereau's *Abduction of Psyche*. A divinely tranquil, gentle breeze comes over the mountains and wraps Psyche together with Eros. When you take a look at this painting, you know immediately that Psyche is totally fulfilled. She has been abducted by Eros, the ultimate spiritual connection. This abduction is not a negative, but a positive reaffirming of Eros's love for Psyche. They are a purely spiritual couple both wrapped in deep purple, symbolizing royalty. After their long, arduous time apart from one another, the twin souls are now reunited on earth. Clearly, they have never lost their heavenly bliss.

As I come out of my half-conscious state I realize it is late. I jog to the hotel and jump in the shower to get ready for dinner. I meet Trudy and the group at a restaurant downstairs. All of us are talking, and we agree Delphi is a magical place. We make a toast to the mystical, spiritual city of the Oracle. It is just about midnight when all of us say goodnight.

The sun has just come up over the mountains and a new day begins. My journey through this mythical country is coming to an end. I have my usual Greek yogurt with honey, coffee, and juice, and Trudy and I board the tour bus for the three-hour trip to Athens.

We have arrived at Athens airport, and the people from our group split up. Trudy and I are traveling together to New York. Trudy lives in California so she will be taking another flight once we land in New York. We board our flight and soar up into the air.

Chapter 93

Chris

Southern California opens her arms once again to me, as I arrive in late January of 1999.

I'm staying with Ron and his family for now, and I am eager to get back into the groove and start riding. In early February, with tears in my eyes, I enter the Santa Anita jockeys' room. It's almost a year and a half since I was here last. It is magical: I see my pants, my picture, my cigar box with all my stuff in it—all set up in the corner, the same way it was when I last rode.[lxxv] I am fit as can be, and I know the trainers see I have the tiger back in my eyes.

Ron tells me I am well liked, and owners and trainers will ride me again. It's going to take some time since people know my history. I am determined, however. I begin to pick up some mounts, and it feels great.

A week and a half later on February 11, 1999, a $62,500 claiming race is off and running. There is a disqualification; the second-place horse is moved up to first, and Chris McCarron is in the irons. No one in his right mind thinks twice about the horse named Charismatic that placed first. As a matter of fact, if you wanted this three-year-old, you could buy him right now for $62,500.

A few days go by and I guide home my first winner, but I am still trying to prove I am here to stay. People know just a year ago I was a down-and-out, overweight jockey. I have a goal to ride in the Kentucky Derby again. I don't care what horse I ride. I just want to be at Churchill Downs on the first Saturday in May. Ron thinks it's a long shot for me to even get a mount on this honored day in racing.

On April 3, I am scheduled to ride Walk That Walk in the Santa Anita Derby. Walk That Walk finishes fifth behind the chestnut that ran in the claiming race just two months ago. General Challenge wins, Prime Timber is second, and Desert Hero is third. My horse does not meet the qualifications to run in the Derby. The Kentucky Derby is less than a month away, and I still do not have a mount.

Then on a quiet Friday afternoon, two weeks after the Santa Anita Derby, I'm riding a horse for trainer Wayne Lukas and I bring home a winner for him. In the winner's circle, Wayne asks me to watch the Lexington Stakes tomorrow. Wayne says, "This colt of mine is coming into his own, and I would like you to ride him in the Derby."[lxxvi] Wayne has already asked top riders like Laffit Pincay Jr., Chris McCarron, Mike Smith, and Jerry Bailey, all of whom have other commitments.

Wayne says that he knew I had a passion to get back.[lxxvii] The next day I'm in the jock's room, watching the Lexington Stakes in Keeneland, Kentucky, on a big screen. Jockey Jerry Bailey is on Wayne's chestnut colt. I look at the racing form, and notice I finished fifth behind this horse in the Santa Anita Derby.

As I'm watching the race, I see the horse has heart. He passes all the other horses down the stretch, and wins by two lengths. Charismatic sets a record for the race, and the record still holds today. I am excited; I have a shot, even if it is a long shot, to win the Kentucky Derby again. I call Ron, and I tell him to speak to Wayne and tell him we are riding Charismatic in the Kentucky Derby. I notice the first six letters of Charismatic rearranged could spell Chris A.[lxxviii] I tell Ron a couple of days later I know who is going to win the Derby.

Ron asks, "Who is it?"

I say, "I had a night vision: we won."[lxxix]

Ron didn't appreciate this intuitive wisdom, and says, "You shouldn't tell anyone—they might think you're crazy."[lxxx] Charismatic is such a long shot that Ron thinks it would take divine intervention for him to cross the wire first.

Chapter 94

Serena

The plane has touched ground in New York, and Trudy and I say good-bye. I say to Trudy, "Let's keep in touch."

She says, "Absolutely." Trudy proceeds to her gate for her flight to California, and I take a taxi home. I slide into my apartment. I hit my pillow, and fall right to sleep.

The next morning I wake up and follow my work routine. I have about eight people to work out today. Spring has sprung in New York, so it is a pleasure to be outside with my clients.

The day turns to night and Chris Antley is in my dreams again. This time we are playing ping-pong, and he wins. I wake up and wonder why I am still having night visions about Chris Antley.

About two weeks go by and my statue of Aphrodite arrives from Greece. I open the huge box, and there she is all in her glory: the goddess of love. The following day I'm at a client's home, patiently waiting for her to get ready. A copy of *Long Island Newsday* is on her table.

I turn to the horse racing section of the paper, and I'm curious about the field for the Kentucky Derby. I notice Chris is not on any horse. Don't ask me why I looked to see the field for the Derby. I haven't been interested in knowing who was in the Derby in years.

≈

Chapter 95

Serena

The Kentucky Derby is not just a horse race; it's an occasion. It is one of the oldest sporting events in the United States, going back to the late 1800s. It was the vision of Colonel Meriwether Lewis Clark Jr., better known as Lutie, who was born on January 27, 1846 in Louisville, Kentucky. He was the grandson of William Clark (of the Lewis and Clark Expedition).

His parents were Meriwether Lewis Clark, and Abigail Prather Churchill. After Lutie's mother died when he was six, he was sent to live with an aunt and uncle. Lutie's uncles, John and Henry Churchill, cultivated in the boy an interest in horse breeding. Lutie married young, and his father-in-law was a breeder and horse trainer. At the age of twenty-six, Lutie traveled to Europe and attended two prestigious horse races: the Epsom Derby and the Grand Prix de Paris.

The English and French played up these races as very happening events, where the royals and the elite would dress to the nines and mingle, eat, and gamble. Lutie was very impressed with the events and thought about a similar idea for Louisville, Kentucky. When Lutie returned to Louisville, he convinced his uncles to lease him some land they owned, and his dream of building his racetrack was on its way to becoming a reality. Lutie formed the Louisville Jockey Club and Driving Park Association. He had good business sense, and sold 320 subscriptions for one hundred dollars per share. Lutie became president of the Jockey Club and Driving Park Association. On May 7, 1875, the first Kentucky Derby was off and running.

A crowd of ten thousand came out and witnessed Aristides win, out of a field of fifteen three-year-old thoroughbreds. For the next twenty years, Lutie, who was an excellent marketer, created an extravagant experience for high society. Despite the event's social success, the Louisville Jockey Club and Driving Park Association fell into financial trouble. Lutie was a rebel, and he would get into gunfights. The people of Louisville did not have much respect for Lutie, and his uncles eventually had enough of Lutie's out-of-control behavior.

The citizens of Louisville started calling the Louisville Jockey Club, Churchill Downs. By 1883 almost everyone was calling the track Churchill Downs. By 1894 Lutie's uncles fired him as president, and sold the land to a Louisville bookmaker. The new owner built a new grandstand, and added two twin spires. The track was still losing money at the end of the nineteenth century, but in the twentieth century, the racetrack's financial state would change.

On April 22, 1899, Lutie shot and killed himself. What a shame. We still owe thanks to this man who gave us the official drink of the Derby, the Mint Julep. He also introduced pari-mutuel betting machines to Kentucky. But the most celebrated accomplishment Lutie gave the United States is that illustrious, distinguished, well-known horse race: the Kentucky Derby!

Chapter 96

Serena

I live in Ray Barone's neighborhood from *Everybody Loves Raymond.* I'm in my apartment in Lynbrook. It is Saturday, May 1, 1999. This is the year we are supposed to party like we've never partied before. It has been said that in a couple of months the world as we know it will change when the Y2K virus comes into effect. If the technical experts can't figure out a solution, our computers will think it is the year 1900. If our machines think it is the beginning of the twentieth century, our modern world will turn upside. This is also the year some think the world will come to an end.

For me, the year 1999 will bring me an amazing present. A blue moon is high in the night sky, as this is the second full moon in a month. As the saying goes, a very rare occurrence is something that happens once in a blue moon. I will be given a gift that will crystallize my connection between the intangible and the tangible. A true spiritual soul mate will manifest before my eyes due to a direct intervention of a force superior to my personality.

It is around one o'clock in the afternoon and I am sitting on my lounge chair. It is a sunny, beautiful day in New York, and the temperature is in the eighties, so I'm thinking about going to the beach to soak up some rays. As I am looking through the television guide, I see an ad with a horse and jockey on it. It is advertising the Kentucky Derby. I realize that today is the first Saturday in May.

The Derby has been running on the first Saturday of May for over one hundred years. *I have not seen a Derby since 1995, and I don't have a conscious clue why I want to watch the Derby this year. I just feel I should view the race today.*

Chapter 97

Chris

The full moon in Scorpio is setting in the west, and we are about to experience life on an intense, deep level. The sun is rising in the east, and it is the start of a new day. All eyes will be here in Louisville, Kentucky, for the Run for the Roses. Ladies who attended this famed race in the early twentieth century were given a red rose. Hence, the red rose became the official race flower.

Churchill Downs is quiet. Horses are galloping around the oval for their morning workouts. Trainers are sipping coffee at the rail, watching their majestic creatures. In a few hours, the quietness of Churchill Downs will give way to the most exciting two minutes in sports.

One hundred fifty-one thousand people will be in attendance for the 125th running of the Kentucky Derby. Women will be dressed in their designer outfits, with matching fancy hats. Men will be in their tailored suits, looking like they just stepped out of nineteenth-century Europe. The great former heavyweight champion of the world, Muhammad Ali, the financial tycoon and future President and First Lady of the United States, Donald Trump and Melania Knauss,Vice-President Al Gore, and his wife Tipper, are just a few of those who will be in attendance for today's race.

The temperature is in the seventies and the sky is picture perfect blue. "There has never been better weather. Welcome to the final Kentucky Derby of the twentieth century," ABC commentator Al Michaels says.[lxxxi] A field of nineteen horses will be running in this year's Derby. General Challenge and Excellent Meeting are the favorites. They are trained by the same trainer, and will be a joint entry as 2 and 2b. Stephen Got Even is the second choice. Worldly Manner has been shipped to Kentucky from the United Arab Emirates. The Crown Prince of Dubai is looking for a Kentucky Derby win with his dark brown colt.

Hank Goldberg and Al Michaels report that Charismatic ran in a claiming race just a few months ago. Hank doesn't think Charismatic has any shot at winning, or even coming in the money.

The time is here. The royal thoroughbreds are making their way from their barns on the backside to the paddock. In the jockey's room, riders are putting their jockey silks on and will be wearing the owner's colors. Zephyr is blowing from the west and the jockey's valets are bringing their rider's saddles to the horses. The trainer and valet are saddling these magnificent equines, and then they will be majestically strutting around the ring until their riders are up.

I step out of the jockey's room wearing green and yellow. I skip to the paddock, and I shimmy to Charismatic's stall. I see trainer Wayne Lukas and the owners of Charismatic, Bob and Beverly Lewis. I say hello to Bob, and I tell Wayne, "We'll get it done."[lxxxii]

The paddock judge calls *riders up.* Wayne gives me a leg up onto Charismatic's back. The other riders are on their respective mounts. Charismatic's groom is leading me to the lead pony, and we are off onto the track for the post parade.

I just heard the sound of the bugle call, letting everyone know the horses are about to come onto the track. As I enter onto the track, there is a collective enthusiasm that brings tears to my eyes. I am overwhelmed, for at this moment the fans are yelling with an electrifying force, while the University of Alabama marching band plays "My Old Kentucky Home." I am just so happy to be here after the hell I suffered to get back.

Chapter 98

Serena

I decide to view the Kentucky Derby at my mother's. I call up Mommy Dearest and I ask her if she wants to have dinner, and she says "Yes."

I order fish at a restaurant and bring the food to my mother's house. I tell my mother, "I want to watch the Kentucky Derby." She agrees. I turn on the television, and on the screen are a list of the horses and jockeys. I am looking at the entries, and I see a horse named Charismatic, and I notice Chris Antley is riding him.

I exclaim, "Oh my God, he is going to win this race." I absolutely know he is going to win. I don't think about placing a bet. I am just overwhelmed by the fact that Chris is riding. I have been dreaming about him for the past year and a half. Then, just a couple of weeks ago, I took note he did not have a mount in today's race.

Now, my mind is focused on Chris and Charismatic. I can see he is on a long shot, but deep down I know he is going to win the 125th Kentucky Derby. The commentators on ABC do not like Charismatic at all, but it doesn't matter what they say. I know he is going to win!

≈

Chapter 99

Chris

The emotional high of the post parade is over, and now I need to be so focused. My lead pony is bringing Charismatic and me into a nice gallop. I feel he is warming up great, and I know we have a good shot. He just needs to break out of the gate well. It is now one minute until post time, and the horses are nearing the starting gate. Charismatic is number eleven. This number represents a channel to the unconscious, and it is charged with charisma and inspiration.

A few days ago at the Derby lottery, we drew post seventeen. There was a late scratch so we will be coming out of the sixteenth hole, way on the outside. Being in the auxiliary gate on the extreme outside is not the best place. The most desirable position is to be in the main starting gate somewhere in the middle of the pack. We have to make up a lot of ground, but there is not much I can do about where we are going to break. I have to just go with the flow. Eighteen of us are carrying 126 pounds. The filly Excellent Meeting has 121 pounds on her back.

The nineteen horses are in the gate and are ready to run on this fast track. The enthusiastic announcer Dave Johnson will call the celebrated, mile-and-a-quarter horse race.

And they're off in the 125th running of the Kentucky Derby! Charismatic breaks sharply, Answer Lively is alive on the inside, Cat Thief is running like he just stole your beloved pet, and Worldly Manner is a worldly horse in front, passing the magic wire the first time. Now Valhol has some energy and takes charge.

On the outside Cat Thief with Mike Smith is second, on the inside Answer Lively is responding in third, Stephen Got Even is getting even in fourth, Desert Hero is seeing a mirage in fifth, Worldly Manner surrounded by palm trees on the outside is sixth, and they are all bunched up at the first turn. Three Ring is circling on the inside, Valhol is leading, Charismatic seems to drop back—come on boy, you know we have this race. We're eighth outside on the backstretch in good position.

Cat Thief is hissing in second, Worldly Manner is third, Stephen Got Even is fourth, Answer Lively is fifth, Desert Hero needs water in sixth, on the inside Three Ring is ninth, in the middle of track Vigor is tenth, First American, Prime Timber, Adonis, Ecton Park, followed by Menifee, General Challenge with Gary Stevens and Excellent Meeting are fourth and third to last, Lemon Drop Kid is eighteenth, and then far back K One King!

Halfway on the turn, moving through, Cat Thief has the lead, now here comes Worldly Manner who resides in the Middle East and tests the leaders, Worldly Manner puts a head in front, Cat Thief at the rail, Charismatic is moving powerfully, come on Charismatic. I feel confident because I haven't set down on him yet.[lxxxiii]

DOWN THE STRETCH THEY COME! Cat Thief thrusting on the inside, Mike Smith, thinking he is on his way to winning, but here comes Charismatic.[lxxxiv] Worldly Manner puts his head in front, but Charismatic is driving hard on the outside. Come on boy, let's switch leads and show the world what we have.

I'm going to show you my whip and tap a few times on the rump to tell you, let's move, and now CHARISMATIC IS TAKING COMMANDING CHARGE and on the inside Cat Thief…

IT IS CHARISMATIC AT THE WIRE by a neck! At the finish line I raise my left hand pointing my index finger to the sky, thanking heaven. Chris Antley on Charismatic wins the Kentucky Derby! Menifee, driving on the outside, was second and Cat Thief was third.

Chapter 100

Serena

A strong force pulls me to pay attention and witness this year's Kentucky Derby. As I am observing the race, I am focusing on Chris and Charismatic. I am following Charismatic all around the racetrack. Down the stretch they come and Charismatic and Chris are in front. I am yelling, "He is going to win this race!" He does! Chris wins with Charismatic. My mother asks, "Why didn't you bet?"

I answer, "I don't know."

Chris just won the 125th running of the Kentucky Derby. I am so ecstatic, and numb at the same time. It is truly an "Oh my God," moment, an unbelievable feat. *I knew Chris was going to win and he did. I just remembered that while I was in Athens, I noticed the Greek statue of a horse in full gallop with his rider pointing his left index finger, as if he had just won a race. I feel I just stepped out of ancient Delphi, and foretold this moment. At the wire, Chris raised his finger to the sky, pointing to the Divine. Chris was given a gift from heaven to win this race for me.*

The name Charismatic comes from the Greek word *charismata*, one who receives spiritual presents. I was given the special ability to know Chris was going to win, and that knowledge is beyond the ordinary. There was no rhyme or reason why I decided to watch the race. All the forces of the universe came together so I could be presented with a profound, divinely-inspired vision.

Chapter 101

Chris

Charismatic and I are in the winner's circle.

I can't believe this is real. I can't contain the adrenaline flow right now.[lxxxv] I just won the Kentucky Derby! I'm in a state of shock, and it feels good.[lxxxvi] Charismatic's groom leads me into the winner's circle. I see Bob Lewis and I jump off of Charismatic, flying through the air. Bob shouts "Unbelievable!"[lxxxvii] I give Bob a big hug. I leap back onto Charismatic's back, and a blanket of roses is draped over the horse's neck.

Charismatic and I are getting our picture taken at this 125th running of the Kentucky Derby. God gave me the Kentucky Derby today; I don't know how to thank the ruling spirit.[lxxxviii] Charismatic's name comes from the Greek, and means, "One who receives spiritual gifts." I am thirty-three years old, and the number 33 is a symbol signifying the spiritual uplifting of the world.

God is in each and every one of us. Something was growing inside me without me realizing what that was. I love every minute of it. I'm living in a miracle; I really am.[lxxxix] I feel an overwhelming happiness, knowing that the most cherished place inside me is connected to an invincible exalted force.

Do you know what it feels like to win the Kentucky Derby? Emotions are powered by the moon. I have the moon in Cancer, which means I am nurturing. I care, I love home life, and I am sensitive.

So how does it feel to win the Kentucky Derby? The first time I won I couldn't say. Now I know what the answer is: it is serene. I feel like a child who's been running from monsters or been afraid or lost for a long time, and who has finally found his mother.[xc]

It is not necessarily your biological mother who can give you this sense of peace. If you didn't have a mother who can give you this feeling, you can get this emotion through a sense of oneness with your immortal being. My mind, body, and soul are for one brief moment in time untroubled. I am one with Charismatic as I am in union with the divine force of the universe. It feels so secure and safe, being in this state.

I can see the awe-inspiring illumination of the full moon in the distance. This powerful time of the year is when the people of Asia are celebrating *Wesak,* Buddha's birth and enlightenment. This auspicious week can bring spiritual knowledge upon the earth, just as we witnessed today! To aspire to reach Buddha in our nature is when we can reach a tranquil mind, and it can extend into the universe.

This was a dream. It set up for me as we approached the quarter pole; I was three, four deep and felt confident. From that point, a rider just hopes nobody will come and get you. Miracles were made to come true. This is the greatest sport there is. It is the Sport of Kings.[xci]

Chapter 102

Serena

I am aroused from a light sleep. *The universe is giving me a gift, as I am serendipitously connected with Chris.* The Kentucky Derby is history now, and Chris Antley is in the news again. It is not coincidental I was dreaming of him, and now I hear about his life and what he has been up to.

Chris has not been riding for the past year and a half, exactly the time slot I started to dream about him. For the rest of the night I am so elated from my prophetic vision. I leave my mother's house and immediately call a friend.

"Hello Nicky!" I scream with joy, "Oh my God, I was dreaming about this jockey I was spellbound with years ago, and he just won the Kentucky Derby."

She says, "Wow, that's very exciting!"

I say, "I just can't believe it."

When I go home, I turn on my computer and start to read. Chris says that he has been overweight and trying to reduce for the past year. He talks about the race and how he received a clean trip. He can't believe it either that he just won the Kentucky Derby.

Morning is here, after an awful night. I am so wound up my mind is going round and round. I jump out of bed and walk up the block to buy the newspaper. I immediately read about yesterday's victory and Chris's life.

Chris talks about how he didn't have any self-worth in the past. The drugs helped him cover up his pain. I am absorbing the information, and remember the intense interactions we had in the past. It's all starting to make sense: Chris is one of my soul's mates. *Oh my God, it is Chris*, I keep saying to myself. One of the gifts I am receiving from the Greek meaning of Charismata is being endowed with the realization of close spirits one is associated with. I am waking up to the knowledge that our souls are connected.

I am thirty-three years old, just like Chris. The number 33 is a very important symbol to spiritually wake up our social order. I am starting to realize that when Chris and I were crossing paths years ago, my personality was semi-conscious of our tie. Now that I have been spiritually awakening over the years, I am fully conscious of the link between us. I feel Chris was spiritually more aware than I was in the past. Our intense encounters stimulated us to wake up the other.

I feel Chris has received his crown, and his third eye has been open since he was born. I on the other hand did not acquire my tiara until much later, and my third eye has been opening little by little, each year I walk on this earth.

Oh my God, the dream I had last year, riding horses in the countryside—it makes sense. I am also remembering what my father said to me years ago. *My father knew a part of him was on earth before. The two immortal beings I am connected to are my father and Chris. We have a common bond—our love of horses and racing.*

Chapter 103

Chris

The trophies are being presented to the owner, trainer, and jockey of Charismatic.

As I accept this symbol of achievement, I want to say something to my family and friends back in South Carolina. They watched me get to this road, and this is the hardest thing I did in my life.[xcii]

I was starting to obtain an emotional foundation being home in South Carolina. My personality was in the right frame of mind. I also had to reach for my soul to come back. I am so glad I am here; I'm still kind of in awe.[xciii]

Charismatic pays $64.40 to win, $27.80 to place, and $14.40 to show. Bob and Beverly Lewis receive $886,200 for winning the Derby. I receive ten percent of the purse.

I had a great career. I had everything in the world. But everything slowly was slipping out of my hands. Everyone has that plague eating at him, that feeling of despair. The world isn't all just roses. There are so many hidden things. Some people just know how to play it better. Some can hide it longer.[xciv]

Have I finally gained emotional security? I was able to get in touch with my will for a short period of time and make a comeback. I had my mind and emotions working together, so that I had the power to make a wise choice. Will I be able to sustain this feat? Only time will tell. What about my weight? Can I sustain reducing every day?

For now I am soaking up the glory of winning the Kentucky Derby again. If Charismatic comes back from this race OK, we are on our way to Baltimore, Maryland. The second leg of the elusive Triple Crown will be upon us.

Chapter 104

Serena

It's all starting to make sense to me. Chris has the same issues as I have with low self-worth. When Chris and I were crossing paths, I thought he did not want to talk to me because I was not worth much. I did not realize he was feeling the same way.

People assume when we reach a certain level of success, we automatically are whole, functioning individuals. Making money and being on the top are only one aspect of our lives. If we don't *feel* our worth from the inside then it really doesn't matter what we have on the outside.

Here I am with all this profound information at my doorstep. Chris and I are connected at our intangible inner essence. Our personalities in the past exuded low self -worth. Do I think I have finally achieved it? I think I have. But do I feel it? The answer is no, but I am not aware of this in this moment.

In a couple of days the second leg of the Triple Crown will be here. Charismatic will be running, and I have been praying to the universe and lighting candles for them. I am hoping Chris and Charismatic will be in the winner's circle at Pimlico.

≈

Chapter 105

Serena

Approximately 340 days after Summer Squall and Bali Babe mated, a gorgeous chestnut red colt was born, on March 13, 1996 in Versailles, Kentucky. He is blessed with the markings of a star between his eyes that extends into a stripe right down the middle of his face. He is also cursed, as his legs below his ankles are white. Because there is only skin, bone, ligaments, cartilage, and tendons below his knee, he can be prone to injury with four white socks.

In due time the foal and his mother will be weaned from each other. It is not a pleasant experience. The mother and her baby have been eating and sleeping together for the past six months. Both mother and child will kick and whine for a few days, but eventually their pain will subside. They need to go their separate ways, maybe to breed again, and for the colt to be broken, so he can be off to the races.

The chestnut is sold for $210,000 to Bob and Beverly Lewis before he is weaned from Bali Babe. Once he is apart from his mother, he is sent to another farm to be broken. A horse is not born accustomed to being saddled, so he needs to be broken in, to accept saddle and rider. This training takes place once a horse is a yearling.

The red horse is one of thousands of yearlings in training. In January 1998, Beverly Lewis names her chestnut colt Charismatic[xcv], just as I am about to start to dream about Chris Antley. Is this a coincidence? I would say yes, because the elements of this occurrence have an interrelationship.

Charismatic's great-grandfather on his mother's side is the legendary Secretariat. Charismatic's father, Summer Squall, won the 1990 Preakness Stakes.

On a sweltering August balmy night in Saratoga in the year 1868, after the races, a group of sportsmen gather at the famed

Union Hall Hotel. One of the men suggests a race be run in honor of this dinner party. The two-mile race to be run by three-year old colts and fillies will be known as the Dinner Party Stakes.

Maryland's governor Oden Bowie is present at this exclusive dinner. Mr. Bowie surprises the men in attendance with a request to make the prize fifteen thousand dollars, a tremendous amount in the nineteenth century. Governor Bowie says he wants the race to be run in Maryland. He feels so passionately about the sport of horse racing that he built a racetrack to honor the Dinner Party stakes.

The birth of Pimlico Race Course is thus decided, and in the autumn of 1870, Pimlico opens, with the Dinner Party Stakes as its highlight. A large dark bay horse named Preakness, one of two colts in a seven-horse field, is the winner.

A very interesting event takes place in the race when a wire is stretched across the track to the judge's stand. Tied to the end of the wire is a bag, and the winning jockey on Preakness claims the bag and the money. This is the start of the term "wire" meaning finish line, and "purse" for the money claimed by the winner.

In the spring of 1873, two years before the Kentucky Derby is first run, Governor Bowie introduces his race as the Preakness Stakes. It has dropped from a two-mile race to a mile and a half, in honor of the Dinner Party Stakes.

Chapter 106

Chris

In the early morning on May 15, 1999, Pimlico is serene. Horses are getting their daily exercise. The track is labeled fast, and moisture is rising from its surface. Just on the dawn of a new moon, the scene creates a very mystical experience.

Owners, trainers, jockey agents, and racing writers have awakened from a night's rest. They are at the rail of the racetrack watching the thoroughbreds gallop. Exercise riders have a tight hold of the reins on these powerful animals. Their riders know if they ask their horse to run they will.

Today is a special day in Maryland: the 124th running of the Preakness Stakes. In a few hours, racing fans will pack the infield, grandstand, and clubhouse of Old Hilltop. Old Hilltop is the nickname for this track where in times past, trainers and racing fans gathered at the small peak in the infield. The Kentucky Derby winner Charismatic has been training strong all week. Most horse people and handicappers don't believe he has a shot at winning the Preakness. They feel Charismatic winning the Derby was a fluke. Menifee, the horse that was driving towards the finish in the Derby, is the favorite for the Preakness.

The sun is shining, and a cool breeze is enveloping the track. Temperatures are in the low seventies. About one hundred thousand people are starting to enter the racecourse. The ladies are wearing their elegant dresses and unique hats, and gentlemen are in their suits. The fans in the infield are dressed casually and are going to have a good, old-fashioned party.

The races begin, and everyone is having a fabulous time. In the seventh race, about two hours before the second jewel of the Triple Crown is to be run, a crazy fan from the infield jumps onto the track as the horses are in a full, driving gallop. Luckily the jockeys see this guy, and no one is hurt. This is not a smart move by this partying man, as jockeys and horses could have been seriously injured.

It's now thirty-five minutes until post time for the Preakness Stakes. Thirteen horses are leaving their barns on the backside. In ten minutes, they will be in the paddock and ready to be saddled.

For this very special race, the entries will be saddled in the wide-open infield, with the exception of Charismatic and Cat Thief. Trainer Wayne Lukas, who just got inducted into the racing Hall of Fame, will be saddling his horses inside just like for any other race.

As of right now Charismatic is fifth choice at the betting window. Menifee is the favorite, with Cat Thief second choice, and then Excellent Meeting. I come out of the jockey's room dressed in the green and yellow silks of Bob and Beverly Lewis.

I make my way to the inside paddock, and I see Bob and Wayne. I shake their hands and before I know it, I hear the call for riders up. Wayne gives me a leg up onto Charismatic. Right away I am connecting with my horse's energy, and we are one. I feel he is ready for this race.

Joe Kelly blows his bugle, and the call to the post has begun. We are on the track for the post parade, and all of us, except the filly Excellent Meeting, will be carrying 126 pounds. The filly will be carrying 121 pounds. I hear the US Naval Academy Glee Club playing the state song "Maryland, My Maryland."

Charismatic is loosening his muscles, as our lead pony is right beside us. I have a microphone attached to my helmet and commentator Al Michaels asks me, "What's the best way to get to the winner's circle Chris?"[xcvi]

I explain for the benefit of sports fans listening to the pre-race coverage. To start off with we need a good break. If he leaves the gate running and I find a good position around the first turn, we have a good shot. He is warming up great, and he is getting into the bridle. He is ready for the performance.

Al says to me, "Good luck."

I say, "Thank you very much."[xcvii]

The thirteen horses are in the gate. Since 1925, the Preakness is run at one mile and three-sixteenths, a sixteenth of a mile shorter than the Derby. It is now post time, and Dave Johnson calls the race.

And they're off in the 124th running of the Preakness. Mike Smith sends the hissing Cat Thief to the lead, Vicar is showing some enthusiasm, and Adonis wants to look good, Kimberlite Pipe is on the rail. Around the first turn, Kimberlite Pipe has the flow, and Cat Thief is running like he is guilty. Vicar is on the outside, Valhol is fourth, Torrid Sand is hot and whirling on the inside fifth, Kimberlite Pipe is on the rail, Cat Thief between horses, these three are inches apart, and then it is another of five lengths to Torrid Sand who is blowing on the inside.

Valhol is right there, the Middle Easterner Worldly Manner is fourth, Valhol fifth, Torrid Sand sixth, Adonis seventh, Menifee eighth, Stephen Got Even ninth, Charismatic is tenth, come on boy, we are in a good position. Badge, Patience Game and Excellent Meeting are last. They are on the backside and Kimberlite Pipe has the lead, but now Cat Thief is running to take commanding charge. Kimberlite Pipe is second, Vicar third…

Charismatic and Chris Antley are driving, Charismatic is fourth, now he is third, but Cat Thief still has the lead. On the top of the stretch, Chris Antley is down low on Charismatic. Oh no, Charismatic! We are going too wide. OK, now we have to get back on track. Let's switch leads, boy. Yes, we are one, and I am riding you, whipping from left to right to get you to win.

We have the lead, Charismatic. Down the stretch we come. Charismatic, we have it now. I am going to hand ride you to the wire. And yes, we did it! I raise two fingers to heaven to symbolize the feat! Menifee is way back in second, Stephen Got Even and Badge are neck and neck, battling it out, but Badge is third. CHARISMATIC AND CHRIS ANTLEY WIN THE PREAKNESS!

Chapter 107

Serena

On this earthy, sensual new moon in Taurus, I have been praying to the divine energy of the universe. I am lighting candles for Chris and Charismatic to win the Preakness. It is May 15, and I'm relaxing on my big black lounge chair in my apartment. I'm nervously waiting for the race to begin. My beautiful Collie is with me, and he is an older dog now. At fifteen, he spends his time lying on fluffy comforters.

It is now post time for the 124th running of the Preakness. I notice it is a beautiful sunny day in Maryland. I am focused on Chris, and I am watching Charismatic's every step to the post parade. The horses are nearing the gate.

The announcer calls they're off! I am so anxious—I want Chris to win so much. I'm grateful as I'm fully awakened now to our deep spiritual connection. I notice he is in the back of the pack on the backside. I'm yelling, "Stay relaxed Chris, and then you can make your move!" At the top of the stretch, I witness Chris driving Charismatic, I'm shouting, "Come on Chris, you can do it!"

Down the stretch they come! I see they are going wide—oh no. But then he straightens out, and I'm ecstatic, gleefully shouting, "Come on, Chris! You can do it!" I am frantic with joy that Chris and Charismatic are going to win. They hit the wire in an easy three-length victory. Chris raises two fingers to heaven: he intuitively knows the force is with him!

I am so consumed with excitement he won! I am hugging Romeo, and I'm yelling out loud, "He won!" It feels so wonderful to me that my soul's mate is on his way to winning the Triple Crown. Chris is exclaiming, "I wish you could jump inside my body right now to know how good I feel."[xcviii] As I share the same inner essence with him, I feel as good as he feels at this moment in time. Chris and Charismatic are coming to New York in three weeks for the Belmont Stakes. The divine energy is with us as I am praying and lighting candles for them to win the Triple Crown.

Chapter 108

Chris

The Preakness is over and I won, and I want to thank the Divine again for giving me a very unique gift. I am pulling up Charismatic, and the head lead pony takes a hold of us. Al Michaels is on the microphone again.

Al says to me, "You liked the way he was warming up before the race, Chris."

I explain to the announcer that Charismatic broke well and I was going to settle him around the second turn. Everybody was jockeying for position outside of me. I chose to take hold, and it was a good, honest pace.[xcix]

Down the backside I had a lot of horse. The whole way Gary Stevens was outside of me. He didn't have a lot of horse at that time at the three-eighths pole. He gave me a shot to get out. I thank Gary for that.

Mr. Michaels observes that it was a powerful move I made around the turn. He says, "It was very charismatic."[c]

As I turn for home, and we go toward the winner's circle, I look up to the Divine to give thanks. Bob Lewis sees us and shouts "That was fantastic!"[ci] Mr. Lewis grabs Charismatic's bridle and leads us into the awesome circle. A blanket of black-eyed Susans, the state flower, is draped over Charismatic's neck, as I put on my lucky baseball cap.

I jump off Charismatic's back, and I am whisked to the platform for the trophy presentation. I see my father and my step-mom Annie on the platform and they give me a hug. Maryland's governor, Parris Glendening, presents the Woodlawn Vase to Bob and Beverly Lewis.

The Woodlawn Vase is named after a Kentucky racecourse that opened in 1859. A wealthy horse breeder contacted Tiffany's to design the trophy, which was created in 1860.

The Woodlawn Racetrack closed during the Civil War, and the vase was buried to keep it safe. Today the sterling silver vase has an estimated value of four million dollars. It is the symbol of victory for the Preakness Stakes, and for this one day, is brought out of hiding from the Baltimore Museum of Art, escorted by Maryland National Guardsmen. Originally, the vase would get passed down to the winner each year, but now, due to its great value, the winning owner, trainer, and jockey get a replica.

The trophy is presented to Bob and Beverly Lewis. Beverly shouts, "This is unbelievable!"[cii]

Bob says with excitement "Can you believe it? I don't want to acknowledge birthdays anymore, but my seventy-fifth was Wednesday."[ciii]

This is a wonderful gift. The winner gets $650,000 from the one-million-dollar purse. Wayne Lukas accepts his trophy and says he had a little bit of a strut to his step when he came off the track during the week. Charismatic was much more focused all week.[civ]

I am on the platform being very serious. People are telling me to smile and be joyous. I'm trying to take it all in. This is special.[cv] I am presented with the trophy, and commentator Jim McKay says to me, "If you ever fall off again, I'll kill you."

I say, "Jim, I won't."[cvi]

The betting public didn't believe that Charismatic and I could pull it off. We were the fifth choice and paid $18.80 to win, $7.60 to place, and $5.80 to show. I feel now we are earning respect. In three weeks we are on our way to New York, and are going to win the Belmont Stakes. History will be made as we conquer the Triple Crown!

Chapter 109

Serena

Horse racing arrived in North America from England in the year 1665. The south shore of Long Island, New York is the home of New Market racecourse. Two centuries later Jerome Park comes into being through the efforts of two visionaries, stock market investor Leonard Jerome and August Belmont Sr. Mr. Belmont is a politician, financial wizard, and racehorse owner/ breeder.

The Belmont Stakes was named after Mr. Belmont and was inaugurated at Jerome Park in 1867, in which year it was won by Ruthless. In 1889 the race was moved to Morris Park, a racetrack in the Bronx. August Belmont Jr., a Harvard graduate and suave businessman, wants to build the largest racetrack in the United States. Belmont Park in Elmont, just outside of New York City, came into being in 1905 to honor Mr. Belmont's father, August Belmont Sr.

England started its own acclaimed races in 1809, the 2,000 Guineas Stakes, the Epsom Derby, and the St. Leger Stakes. The American races matched those of England's. The term "Triple Crown" did not enter people's minds until the early 1930s.

The Belmont Stakes is the oldest of the Triple Crown races. Called "The Test of Champions," the race is a grueling mile and a half. The length of the race does not seem that long, but these horses train intensely for five weeks. Over the past one hundred years, racehorses have been bred for speed, not stamina. This race is the only time thoroughbreds go this distance. The Belmont is the "Run for the Carnations," symbolizing love and luck. It has been said the first carnation appeared on this Earth when Mary felt the pain and suffering of Jesus, as he was carrying his cross.[cvii]

When a jockey and horse turn for home on the top of the stretch at Belmont Park, it feels like eternity to the wire, as this is the test of all tests. A racehorse is like any athlete: there is the dichotomy between the thrill of victory, and the agony of defeat.

Chapter 110

Chris

Darkness turns into the lightness of day as a rooster crows on the backside of Belmont Park. It is early morning of June 5 as the night watchman in Wayne Lukas's barn feeds Charismatic oats mixed with sweet feed. This will be the most important day of Charismatic's life. Will he gallop into eternity with the eleven other immortal thoroughbreds that have conquered the Triple Crown?

There is a smell in the air signaling the warmth of summer. Trainers, exercise riders, grooms, and hot walkers are making their way into the barns. Horses are going out for their morning gallops around the main track of Belmont Park.

The media is swirling around Wayne Lukas's barn. Racing writers and commentators want a glimpse of the star. I come into the barn to see Charismatic. I woke up early because my thoughts were circling around in my mind.

In a few hours, the sun will be high in the bright blue sky for the 131st running of the Belmont Stakes. People will come from all over—by plane, train, bus, car, and on foot—to witness history being made.

At this moment, Charismatic is making his way onto the track with his exercise rider up for a nice and easy walk around Belmont's oval. Wayne Lukas takes a hold of Charismatic's bridle, as he is on his pony (a non-racing horse) strolling along, absorbing the moment. Wayne wants him to relax, but Charismatic is hyper, as he wants to run. He is a little upset that he may only walk.[cviii]

A few hours later, I drive to the Belmont clubhouse, and make my way into the jock's room. The jockey's room is like a little home for the riders where they can rest, play ping-pong, or jump into the sweatbox.

A crowd of about eighty-three thousand people has gathered at beautiful Belmont Park, which has a laid-back, picnic feel. People can sunbathe on the grass in the grandstand area or can be dressed to the nines in the clubhouse.

The New York Yankees have just defeated the New York Mets, and now Charismatic is going for the Triple Crown. ABC commentator Al Michaels voices with enthusiasm, "Welcome to Belmont Park. One definition of 'charismatic' is the ability to inspire followers with devotion and enthusiasm. This horse has done nothing of the sort until today."[cix]

Charismatic is finally getting respect, as he is the favorite to win the Belmont Stakes. Menifee is the second choice, and the filly Silverbulletday is third in a field of twelve horses. Charismatic's earnings so far are just under two million dollars. With a win today, that total could jump to seven million dollars. This trip to New York has been surreal; yesterday morning I rang the opening bell for the New York Stock Exchange. My weekly stock tips in *The Ant Man Report* are creating quite a following now on the World Wide Web.

I ask myself, "What if I don't win?" The hopes are there. If you ask me if can I win, I will say I can't lose. But I have prepared myself. If I don't claim that sweet victory, I will be OK with what God has given me up to this point; no one can ask for more.[cx]

It is forty-five minutes until post time. Charismatic makes his way to Belmont's gorgeous paddock. I am wearing the famous green and yellow silks, and I weigh in, so the clerk of scales knows the horse will be carrying 126 pounds. Right now, I am at my riding weight of 115 pounds, so to make 126 pounds, weight is added to my saddle.

I am so nervous that I say a prayer to the Divine and stretch my legs before I venture out into the crowd. Charismatic is prancing around the walking ring very excitedly. There are hundreds of people in the paddock. The record crowd seems to be on Charismatic's side.

Charismatic and I are number four, and I go over to Bob Lewis, and shake his hand. Wayne and my valet are saddling Charismatic. The call for riders up has just been announced, and Wayne gives me a leg up. I am very focused as I make my knot in my reins and check my stirrups. We are heading out to the track via a tunnel that connects the paddock to the track.

The bugler blows his trumpet and the sound to the call to the post has been made. Charismatic and I are on the track for the post parade, and the crowd is going wild. The rider on my lead pony takes a hold of Charismatic, and I can faintly hear the Broadway star Linda Eder singing "New York, New York." I see a fan in the grandstand holding up a sign that reads, "Wow." Then I realize I am back in New York—I wonder where my heart-pounding girl has been in all these years? *Get your mind back here Chris*, I say to myself.

The parade is over and now my lead pony and I are going into a nice soft gallop. I have a microphone on me, and I can hear Al Michaels. Al asks, "Chris what are you thinking?"

I tell him I am focusing on the race, running things through my mind. Getting a last minute check up, kind of like when you go up and fly a plane, you go through all the systems and look through the papers to make sure everything is right.[cxi]

Al asks, "How is he warming up?"

"He is warming up fine," I say. "Very relaxed, even though there is a lot of commotion and the crowds are loud."

Al says, "You can hear that crowd right now. Chris, good luck."

"Thank you, Al."[cxii]

It is now post time, and the horses are nearing the gate. Lemon Drop Kid is giving the starters a little trouble getting into the gate but there he goes. Charismatic is very calm and loads like a pro. Dave Johnson is waiting to call the race.

AND THEY'RE OFF! Will Charismatic claim a Triple Crown victory? Menifee is shooting in front and Menifee has the lead, Stephen Got Even is getting even on the outside, and Silverbulletday shoots through. Charismatic is behind her. Charismatic leads, Silverbulletday is grabbing a Coors Light and is second on the rail, Stephen Got Even is not getting even and is back third, Menifee is running fourth, Vision and Verse is seeing 20/20 in fifth, Prime Directive is directing on the outside sixth.

Patience Game is being patient in seventh place, Lemon Drop Kid is next, followed by Teletable, Adonis is not looking so good, five lengths back to Best of Luck, and farther back is Pineaff, the opening half mile in forty-three and one-fifth seconds, the speed is powerful here.

The filly Silverbulletday is shooting her silver bullet and has the lead, Charismatic is right there, Stephen Got Even is third, Vision and Verse has perfect vision fourth, Prime Director is still directing fifth, down the backside, Pat Day on Menifee is within striking range and is only five and half lengths behind Charismatic with five furlongs to go, then it's Lemon Drop Kid, Teletable, Adonis, Patience Game, Best of Luck, it's way back to Pineaff, around the far turn, and the filly is hanging in tough, Silverbulletday is in the lead.

Chris Antley gives Charismatic his cue, as the field comes to the top of the stretch. On the outside Stephen Got Even is third and Vision and Verse is seeing the victory, Lemon Drop Kid is looking to celebrate with a Limoncello Martini on the outside.

DOWN THE STRETCH THEY COME! Charismatic is so desperately trying to hang on to the lead, but Lemon Drop Kid takes command. As they come to the final furlong, Lemon Drop Kid and Vision and Verse, Charismatic is hanging on, but it's Lemon Drop Kid in front and Vision and Verse second. Charismatic has been defeated. Charismatic hangs on for third.

Chapter 111

Chris

I am just past the wire. Oh no, I can sense something is not right with Charismatic. He dips under me[cxiii] and my first instinct is to pull him up. I jump off of him in a heartbeat. I can sense his left front leg is hurt. I can feel his pain so I try to take the weight off his leg. I am holding his leg like I would hold a baby. Within seconds the lead outrider comes over with his horse and grabs a hold of the reins. I comfort Charismatic until the horse ambulance comes and takes him back to his barn.

Tears are rolling down my face. I can't hold back my emotions. I take my saddle off of him and walk to the clerk of scales in a numb state. I am in shock and I don't even hear the crowd feeling for Charismatic, and for me.

Al Michaels says this is the worst conceivable ending.[cxiv] I am inconsolable. Tears are streaming from my eyes. I feel so bad. He gave us a lot. He gave America a lot. It is sad when these things happen.[cxv]

The "run for the carnations" brings home to me the origin of this divine flower. The first carnation appeared on Earth when Mary wept for the pain and suffering for Jesus. The deepest part of me is weeping for the misery and torture of Charismatic, and also for all the people who are in psychological and emotional agony. The crowd is feeling my grief and that of Charismatic. I know deep down all of us have the compassion to open our hearts and feel for ourselves and others.

Charismatic is being loaded in the ambulance and a veterinarian will take x-rays of his leg immediately. The tests show he fractured two bones of his ankle, the bottom of the cannon bone and a sesamoid bone. When a racehorse is in full gallop going close to forty miles per hour, the ankles are absorbing most of the shock. The horse's weight is putting extreme pressure on the foot, as the ankle hits hard on the dirt. In full gallop as the weight is still on the foot, the bones of the ankle are very vulnerable.

Dr. Bramlage says Charismatic will rest for a couple of days and then he will have surgery. He will have screws inserted in his ankle and if all goes well he will live a long life. But his racing career is over.

Some people question my ride. They say I had Charismatic too close to the lead. I let Charismatic run along at his own pace and the colt was relaxed despite showing speed.[cxvi] Wayne says if I had to draw it out on paper I wouldn't have had him that close. But easy as he was running, I didn't have any problem with it. Wayne told me don't fight him, just leave him alone.[cxvii] That is what I let him do. He settled into the bridle, and I had a lot of horse under me.

My dad and step-mom Annie feel so bad for me they just give me a big hug. I feel comforted by their warmth of empathy for me. I am so worried about Charismatic. I hope he pulls through this horrific injury. I am praying to the Divine for his recovery.

Lemon Drop Kid is the winner. Charismatic and I were on restricted number four. Lemon Drop Kid paid $61.50 to win, $26.00 to place, and $10.60 to show. Vision and Verse paid $44.40 to place, and $17.00 to show. Charismatic paid $3.60 to show.

Al Michaels says, "We've said it before and it never rang truer than today. This sport of horse racing features the highest of highs and the lowest of lows."[cxviii]

Chapter 112

Serena

The night before the Belmont Stakes I am praying for Chris to guide Charismatic into history. I wake up the next morning filled with anxiety. To calm my nerves I light candles and say a prayer out into the universe for Chris.

To spend a day at the races is a mind-blowing experience. Crowds of people come together to witness the allure of horse racing. When you see your thoroughbred in front at the top of the stretch, and he crosses the wire first, it is a thrill not to be missed.

Even though I live twenty-minutes from Belmont Park I decide to stay home and view the race. Romeo is lying on a big comforter in my apartment, and I turn on the TV. It is an hour until post time for the Belmont. Chris's step-mom Annie is being interviewed, talking fondly about her stepson: "He had been away his entire adult life. And maybe he didn't have a good feeling about where he fit in. I think just realizing that he was appreciated as a person—Uncle Chris, or Grandson Chris, Nephew Chris, Cousin Chris and Son Chris—not jockey Chris."[cxix]

In these past five weeks I have been consciously waking up to the fact that Chris is a part of my soul. He has been going through the same issues I have been dealing with, as I don't know where I fit in with my family either. Years ago, I was semi-conscious of the fact that we are connected, but now that link is so apparent. *Chris is aware that God is in each and every one of us. Just as I have, he has been getting in touch with his own soul for the past seven years, as our immortal being is part of the divine force of the universe.*

Time has been rolling by, and it is now post time for the Belmont Stakes. I am focused on Chris as the gates open, and I notice they break well. Chris has Charismatic in good striking position. On the top of the stretch I see Chris is already down on

Charismatic asking him to run. I know if one is already driving on the top of the stretch one is probably not going to have that much horse left in the last furlongs. As I expect, down the stretch Charismatic is fading to a third-place finish. But then right after the wire, I see the unthinkable. Chris is pulling Charismatic up, and he jumps off of him. I say "Oh no, what is happening?" Chris is holding Charismatic's leg in the air as the outrider comes over and grabs the reins from Chris.

Moments later, Chris and his valet take his tack off, and Chris is walking on the track crying. I feel for him and Charismatic, and I hope Charismatic is OK. The press is swirling around Chris, and Chris doesn't know what to say; tears are just rolling down his face. I am upset too, and tears are falling from my eyes as well. I just want to hug him, knowing how deeply we are a part of each other.

Chapter 113

Chris

I am very grateful for the opportunity to ride Charismatic, a racehorse imbued with heart and soul.

Charismatic was the underdog and so was I. Before the Derby most people ignored us, but we made history. I thank God for giving me this gift. Dr. Bramlage says the surgery is a success: Charismatic shattered his ankle, but three screws are inserted, and he will live a long and fulfilling life. He will eventually stand at stud in Japan. Maybe he will have the opportunity to create a little Zen in his life.

The veterinarians say I saved Charismatic's life by my quick reaction to jump off of him. I felt his pain, and wanted to help him the best way I knew how. My emotions poured out of me like lava erupting out of a volcano. I felt the pain and suffering of Charismatic and everyone out there.

I continue to ride in top form the rest of the year. I am winning races in California, and am able to keep my riding weight under control. I fly to Saratoga in the summer and win races there as well. In the fall, I travel back to New York and ride Doneraile Court to victory in the Jerome Handicap for now Hall-of-Fame trainer, Nick Zito. I even win two major stakes races at Belmont Park: the Woodward stakes and the Jockey Club Gold Cup, aboard River Keen.

It's now late fall and the Breeder's Cup is here, and throughout my illustrious career I have been given eleven starters on this very special day in racing. My best place finish is on Forestry in the Breeder's Cup Sprint this year.

I feel I need to take some time off right now, as one of my knees is hurting. In a few months I will be attending the Eclipse Award dinner with a friend. This extravagant night is held at the Beverly Hilton in Beverly Hills, California. It's a night to celebrate the outstanding horses, owners, trainers, and jockeys of the year. Charismatic is voted horse of the year for 1999, and Best Moment of 1999 is my quick decision to jump off of Charismatic and hold his leg until help came.

Chapter 114

Serena

Charismatic's Triple Crown run has been overwhelming for me. My spiritual consciousness has been awakened and I realize that Chris is the other half of my soul. There is one problem: my personality is still not up to par with what my soul knows to be true. I feel I still don't have the self-worth to connect with Chris at the personality level.

Still, I decide to find his e-mail address, and I try to voice my knowledge of our connection. It is the end of June and I send an email to him, but I am very vague about telling him who I am and our link. In the next three months, I am consistently looking online and in the newspaper to see how many races he has been winning. I am hoping he responds to my e-mail.

Then on Saturday September 18, the same day Chris wins the Woodward Stakes here in New York, I visit Anabel, my friend who is very intuitive. I explain my story and she says I have to tell Chris about my bond with him.

I am so nervous, but around September 23, I send another e-mail, and I pour my heart out to him.

I tell him I am the girl from New York, and that I used to work at Belmont Park. I remind him that we used to cross paths, and we were mesmerized by each other. I tell him he has been on my mind for the past year and a half.

I write, "I love your eyes—I never forgot your eyes. In the past, I was physically attracted to you, but now I feel there is something more than just a physical attraction. I feel you are the other half of my soul. That's just astronomical. We are a piece of heaven on earth."

Months go by and I don't receive a response, I'm getting frustrated again! In March of 2000, I disconnect from him…

Chapter 115

Chris

March rolls in like a lamb in Southern California. My knee feels better, and I am back in the saddle, picking up a winner here and there. Then on March 19, 2000, I ride a horse named Sixshooter in a six-furlong race. I come in second, and this will be my last race in this lifetime. Here I am, depressed and again struggling to make my riding weight.

Out of 19,723 horses I have mounted in my career, I have 3,480 wins. I have come in second place 2,881 times, and have crossed the wire third 2,494 times. My total purse earnings are $92,261,894.

Months ago, I received an e-mail from the girl who put me in a trance years earlier. She tells me we're connected at the soul level. She is just giving me validation, as I always knew she felt otherworldly to me.

I know I cannot connect with her at my personality level. Have I transformed myself into an emotionally strong person? The answer is "No." I am distraught, as I am now fully conscious about our connection, but I cannot do anything about it. *I am paralyzed by this profound information. And I feel the energy has changed within and around me, these last few weeks and I don't like it.*

What do I do? I grab onto my false security blanket. I rely on my drugs to give me a pick up. I am feeling very lonely and lost, so I find emotional comfort in a woman who has been chasing me for the past nine months.[cxx] I follow my natural instinct to reproduce and she becomes pregnant. I decide to marry her, and on April 12 we tie the knot in Las Vegas in front of a few friends and my family. I believe this is not the first time she has walked down the aisle.[cxxi] I really want to be a father, and know I cannot have my heart-pounding girl.

I am living in an estranged situation. My wife, who is about six feet tall, is in New York and I am in California.[cxxii] I accompany her to the Kentucky Derby in the year 2000. After the Derby we see each other about once a month, and I do not see her at all in the last months of my life.

I unravel emotionally: what have I done? Did my personality make a wise choice? She is spending my money like it is going out of style.[cxxiii] I sink lower and lower as time goes on. *I sense the energy of my beloved soul mate around me again. My immortal being wants my girl who puts me in a trance. My soul cannot go on living, knowing I am connected to her.*

If you desire to mate with a soul mate, you must transcend your emotional pain and suffering. Maybe I'm expressing wisdom that will help someone else. That is the ultimate in life when you can help someone else from making the same mistakes.[cxxiv] Seven and a half months after my wedding, after months of living each day spaced out on drugs, I cross over to the other side.

The coroner discovers I have a severe head injury, and finds four drugs in my system on December 2, 2000, the night I die in my Pasadena, California, home. My immortal being knows I needed to settle the karmic debt with the girl I married. As for my everlasting mate, my soul knows we needed to evolve to our other halves. Our exalted inner beings are extremely close, almost like we are one. *Our love is second only to the love of our other halves.* I am sure her eternal self knows, *we will meet again!*

Epilogue

Serena

As I enter Aqueduct Racetrack in the late morning of December 3, 2000, a strange feeling is within me. Within minutes of my arrival, Connie, my client and friend, says to me, "Chris Antley has died." I go into shock: I have to leave my lunch date and go home. I am traveling on the Belt Parkway going to my apartment in Lynbrook, and I am in a catatonic state. I almost have two collisions with other cars.

I enter my apartment and turn on my computer: right away Chris is making headlines. I just can't believe he died, and to top it all off, I read he married and produced a child (born in January, 2001). Months ago I read he married, but I didn't want to believe it. He got married and produced a child in the weeks, I was separating my energy from him. I wanted him to come towards me, not away from me. I question why my soul and the Divine guided me towards this awakening? What was my knowledge about our connection for? Just to say goodbye? I can't accept what I am experiencing.

What did my connection with Chris mean if we were not going to be together? The pain is so unbearable that I think my soul is going to crack in half. Chris has been in my night visions since the beginning of 1998. I take a long time to fall asleep on this very devastating day, and wake up the next morning feeling like I am going to lose my mind—the agony is cutting through me like someone stabbed my heart with a knife multiple times.

About two weeks after he crossed over, Chris appears in the sweet whispers of my dreams. My father is present in my dreams too. The three of us are at the races, and I see a tunnel and I wave to Chris and my father.

It is New Year's Eve, and snow is falling. As I am cleaning my car off I say out loud, "I know you're here, Chris."

The afternoon of New Year's Eve I am meditating by my bed. I have a mosquito net attached to the ceiling that I never take down, but when I come home after a night with my friends, the net is down. I know Chris's soul has been here.

I am frustrated: my mind is not at peace, and I cannot eat. The first week after his passing, I hardly sleep. I feel all alone. I just lost a slice of my soul. Every night I fall asleep and Chris is there, and I don't want to get up.

All I want to do is stay with my beloved. I must make the choice to get up and carry on with my day, or slip away into the abyss. I choose to get up, but not without a lot of pain. My days consist of going about life sleepwalking for weeks.

Weeks go by and I click on a website Chris's mother set up, telling the world that if anyone knew her son, she would like to hear from them. I e-mail Michelle and she calls me; we talk about Chris, and we start to cry.

Out of the blue, a week before the 2001 Belmont Stakes, Michelle Antley calls me and asks if she can visit. She wants to come to New York for Chris's memorial service, held by the New York Racing Association.

The eve of the Belmont Stakes, I drive to the airport. Inside, I spot Michelle coming down the escalator. As I pull into the driveway of the Garden City Hotel, I notice a bunch of people gathering for the service. I feel grateful I am here, but not fulfilled, because only Michelle knows of my connection to Chris.

After the ceremony, we enter the hotel to have a drink, and hours later we head to my apartment. Morning arrives, and it is a beautiful, sunny, warm day in New York. Michelle and I make our way to Belmont Park in the late afternoon, and we watch Point Given, ridden by Gary Stevens, win the Belmont Stakes.

Exactly a month after the Belmont Stakes, I have to grieve for another soul. Arthritis claims my beloved Romeo. Now seventeen years old, he cannot walk anymore, and has to be put to sleep. I bury him in a pet cemetery on Long Island.

Now I am grieving for two souls, and I do not have peace. What does all this mean? I have to seek help, and I contact a psychotherapist. My therapist is amazed by my story about how Chris and I consciously recognized each other.

I am still so frustrated as to why he could not connect to me through his personality. I e-mailed him again in June of 2000, but my message was returned because of an inoperable address. My therapist confirms his personality was not present. He still did not believe he was worth being loved just for himself. He attracted people into his life because they loved what he represented, like fame and money.

Two weeks after the World Trade Center disasters, I fly to Elloree, South Carolina, and Michelle and I visit Chris's grave along Old Highway 6. There I say a prayer to my beloved soul mate. It takes me almost three years to finally have peace with the realization that Chris and I were never going to connect on a physical level.

I am still recovering from my own dysfunctional issues, so I was not ready to connect at the soul level either. The realization that Chris and I were never going to connect at the third dimensional level, was a test. I understand now he had to balance karma to free his soul to become closer to the Divine. *Chris and I were so close, almost like one soul, our love is second only to the love of our other halves.*

Chris Antley has to be remembered as a person who was intuitively and spiritually astute (a man ahead of his time), and as one of the greatest jockeys who graced the world of horse racing. Chris is one of my soul's mates, just like my father is one of my truest companions, and we are eternally bonded. *What I know for sure is that the three of us will meet again*!

Questions for Discussion

1. Serena Jade has a close bond with her father. How would you describe your relationship with your father? Do you have a common bond between you?
2. The author has a narcissistic mother. Did you ever hear of the term? If so, what did you think it meant? Did you think all mothers give their lives for their children? Are you aware of your psychological and emotional history?
3. Serena Jade and Chris Antley take one look and recognize one another at a very deep level. Before reading *Charismatic Connection*, did you think magical encounters only happened in movies?
4. The author has an amazing journey of self-discovery with her mind, body and soul. Do you think you have the tenacity to stick to such a quest?
5. Serena Jade and Chris Antley are in a lot of emotional pain. Are you aware of your own suffering? If so, how are you going to transform your pain?
6. *Charismatic Connection* brings a positive light to the sport of horse racing. Do you think you would be interested in going to the races on a regular basis?
7. Serena Jade has been to exotic locales. Do you have a desire to travel and embrace our world?
8. Serena Jade was addicted to sex and working out. Chris Antley was addicted to drugs and alcohol. Everyone has an addiction, even if it's to power. What are you addicted to?
9. The author talks about her servant identity. She questions if she will make the transition from servant to empress. Are you the servant, or the royal monarch? If you are the servant, do you have the courage to transform?

10. Serena Jade and Chris Antley have an extraordinary spiritual connection. What was your knowledge about soul mates before you read *Charismatic Connection*?
11. Serena Jade and Chris Antley woke up the other to their deepest nature. Individually, they became aware of the spiritual force inside themselves. How devoted are you to living a life aware of your spiritual identity?

With Thanks

I want to thank with all my heart two important friends in my life, James Canavan and Lenore Giraud. Without you giving me support, I never would have had the faith to pursue my dreams.

I also want to thank my former clients for teaching me how to embrace the empress lifestyle.

Purse $18,000

Belmont Park, New York
Very Un Stable owner
R. O'Connell trainer
Tustunugee 2nd

THEY ARE ALL CRAZY

July 17, 1991
Chris Antley up
6 furlongs time 1:11:2
Northern Puppy 3rd

About the Author

Serena Jade is a psycho-spiritual author, and globe-trotting yoga teacher who blends Freudian/Jungian unconscious dives with a passion for uncovering the mystical origins of soul mates and twin flames. She weaves a mystical & scientific tapestry of Tantra, Sufi, Gnostic, Kabbalah as well as Philosophy of Physics into her repertoire.

She is the author of several books including: Charismatic Connection: Whispers of A Love That Transcends Time. Her works are mainly focused on psychology, religion, and travel. She draws inspiration from Ancient and Modern Mysticism, Joseph Campbell, and Carl Jung. Serena Jade's books, retreats, courses, yoga classes, and coaching are built around the idea of living life exuding wellness and following one's own soul's passion and purpose.

Teaching: As a certified Kundalini Tantra Yoga Instructor, Serena Jade imparts wisdom on raising divine energy and uplifting the body and mind. Her teachings blend laughter, sound healing meditation, restorative, and spiritual practices.

Wellness Advocate: Serena Jade's journey extends beyond books and teachings. She inspires people to explore the world, cultivate physical fitness, balance the mind, and awaken their sixth sense.

Unparalleled Wisdom: Her travels, knowledge, and insight into the highest spiritual attainment make her a beacon of light for those seeking inner transformation.

For more about Serena Jade, check out her website at serenajade.co or explore her company, The House of Raising The Sparks, at TheHouseofRaisingTheSparks.com.

Endnotes

Chapter 4

1. Karyl Mc Bride, *Will I Ever Be Good Enough?: Healing the Daughters of Narcissistic Mothers,* (New York: Free Press, 2000), 8-10.

Chapter 6

2. Lenny Shulman, "The Charismatic Chris Antley," *Bloodhorse.com*, December 4, 2000. http://www.bloodhorse.com/horse-racing/articles/2081/the-charismatic-chris-antley
3. Bettie B. Youngs, *How to Develop Self-Esteem in Your Child*, (New York: Ballantine Books, 1991), 73-83.
4. Bill Finley, "Antley's Career is in Jeopardy," *Chicago Tribune*, October 22, 1989.

Chapter 16

5. Elizabeth Mitchell, *Three Strides before the Wire,* (New York: Hyperion, 2002), 102-110.
6. Ibid.
7. Susan Morris Finley, "Chris Antley at the Crossroads," *The Thoroughbred Record*, April, 1989.
8. ABC Television interview before Preakness, (part 2) 1999: www.youtube.com/watch?v=CFrmfPp2hos
9. Bill Finley, "The Blessed, Yet Cursed Life of Chris Antley," espn.com, April 30, 2001.
10. Susan Morris Finley, "Chris Antley at the Crossroads," *The Thoroughbred Record*, April, 1989.

Chapter 18

11. Ed Fountaine, "Antley's Long, Hard Ride: Jockey Overcomes Demons To Win Derby," *New York Post*, 1999.
12. Susan Morris Finley, "Chris Antley at the Crossroads," *The Thoroughbred Record*, April, 1989.

13. "Horse Racing," *New York Times*, November 17, 1987.
14. Susan Morris Finley, "Chris Antley at the Crossroads," *The Thoroughbred Record*, April, 1989.
15. Elizabeth Mitchell, *Three Strides before the Wire*, (New York: Hyperion, 2002), 102.

Chapter 20

16. Elizabeth Mitchell, *Three Strides Before the Wire*, (New York: Hyperion, 2002), 116–117.
17. Ibid.
18. Ibid.

Chapter 22

19. Alex Tresniowski, "Ridden by Demons," *People Magazine*, January 8, 2001.
20. Gary Stevens, *The Perfect Ride* (New York: Citadel Press-Kensington, 2002), 183.
21. Alex Tresniowski, "Ridden by Demons," *People Magazine*, January 8, 2001.

Chapter 24

22. Susan Morris Finley, "Chris Antley at the Crossroads," *The Thoroughbred Record*, April, 1989.
23. Ibid.
24. Ibid.
25. Ibid.

Chapter 31

26. Ed Fountaine, "Antley's Long, Hard Ride: Jockey Overcomes Demons To Win Derby," *New York Post*, 1999.
27. Ibid.

Chapter 37

28. Susan Morris Finley, "Chris Antley at the Crossroads," *The Thoroughbred Record*, April, 1989.

Chapter 43

29. Susan Morris Finley, "Chris Antley at the Crossroads," *The Thoroughbred Record*, April, 1989.
30. Ibid.

Chapter 45

31. Susan Morris Finley, "Chris Antley at the Crossroads," *The Thoroughbred Record*, April, 1989.
32. Ibid.
33. Ibid.
34. Ibid.

Chapter 47

35. Susan Morris Finley, "Chris Antley at the Crossroads," *The Thoroughbred Record*, April, 1989.
36. Capades. Wikipedia: www.en.wikipedia.org/wiki/Capades.11/12/2011
37. Ed Fountaine, "Antley's Long, Hard Ride: Jockey Overcomes Demons To Win Derby," *New York Post*, 1999.

Chapter 49

38. George Vecsey, "Antley Swings Hot Whip," *New York Times*, 1989.
39. Ibid.
40. Bill Finley, "The Blessed, Yet Cursed Life of Chris Antley," espn.com, April, 2001.
41. Steven Crist, "Antley Receives Ban From Belmont," *New York Times*, September, 1989
42. Andrew Beyer, "Old Story: Athlete Discovers That Cocaine Holds Rein on His Life," *Los Angeles Times*, October 1, 1989.

Chapter 54

43. Lenny Shulman, "Antley Recalled as Talented, Troubled Jockey," *Bloodhorse.com*, December 5, 2000.
44. Joseph Durso, "Strike the Gold Hits Pay Dirt and Wins Derby," *New York Times*, May 5, 1991.

45. 1991 Kentucky Derby – Strike The Gold + post race: www.youtube.com/watch?v=vsXDdnLaZqE
46. Marty McGee, "Hansel's Tale Has Happy Ending," *Baltimore Sun*, May 19, 1991.
47. Joseph Durso, "Hansel Captures Belmont by a Head," *New York Times*, June 9, 1991.

Chapter 57

48. William Nack, "Preakness Winner Hansel Outdueled Kentucky Derby Winner," Sports Illustrated. June 17, 1991.
49. Ibid.

Chapter 61

50. "Mount at Aqueduct Throws Antley," *New York Times*, November 14, 1992
51. Joe Drape, "An Addict With One Weapon: Hope," *New York Times*, May 15, 1999.

Chapter 65

52. Esther Blodgett, *Everything Catskills but the Kitchen Sinks*, (Peter Finn: 2010), 6.

Chapter 67

53. Joe Drape, "Antley Faced His Demons Before Winning the Derby Again," *New York Times*, 1999.

Chapter 68

54. Joseph Durso, "Fourth Place and Farewell to East Coast for Antley," *New York Times*, 1993.
55. Talked to my client's brother, trainer Howard Zucker, in Oceanside, New York, 1994.

Chapter 72

56. Lenny Shulman, "Antley Recalled as Talented, Troubled Jockey," *Bloodhorse.com*, December 5, 2000.

Chapter 77

57. "Antley's Hometown Reflects on Favorite Son," *Bloodhorse.com*, December 7, 2000.

Chapter 83

58. William Nack, "Just six months after his career seemed doomed by a weight problem, Chris Antley rode Charismatic," *Sports Illustrated*, May 10, 1999.
59. June, 2001, talked to Michelle Antley about *Conversations with God.*
60. Neal Donald Walsh, *Conversations with God*, (New York: Putnam's Sons, 1996), back cover.
61. Lenny Shulman, "Antley Recalled as Talented, Troubled Jockey," *Bloodhorse.com*, December 5, 2000
62. Gary Stevens, *The Perfect Ride* (New York: Citadel Press-Kensington, 2002), 180.

Chapter 86

63. Dave Kindred, "Antley's Ride? It Was Charismatic," *Sporting News*, May 10, 1999.
64. Lenny Shulman, "Antley Recalled as Talented, Troubled Jockey," *Bloodhorse.com*, December 5, 2000.
65. Ed Fountaine, "Antley's Long, Hard Ride: Jockey Overcomes Demons to Win Derby," *New York Post*, 1999.
66. Joe Drape, "An Addict with One Weapon: Hope," *New York Times*, May 15, 1999.
67. Ibid.

Chapter 87

68. Patricia Joudry and Maurie Pressman, M.D., *Twin Souls: A Guide to Finding Your True Spiritual Partner*, (New York: Carol Southern Books, 1995), back cover.

Chapter 88

69. Ed Fountaine, "Derby Champ Battled Inner Demons," *New York Post*, December 4, 2000.
70. Neil Schmidt, "Derby Winner, Jockey Beat Long Odds," The Cincinnati Enquirer, May 2, 1999.
71. Elizabeth Mitchell, Three Strides before the Wire (New York. Hyperion, 2002), 324.

Chapter 90

72. Lenny Shulman, *Ride of Their Lives* (Lexington, KY: Eclipse Press, 2002), 31.
73. Steven Michaels, Radio interview on Charismatic, ESPN: The Documentary, (Part 4): www.youtube.com/watch?v=VJhdKDJ1PRM

Chapter 92

74. Plato, trans. Desmond Lee, *Critias* (New York: Penguin Classics, 1971), 140.

Chapter 93

75. "Antley on the Verge of Becoming a Triple Crown Jockey," *Sports Illustrated*, June 3, 1999.
76. Wallace Matthews, "Once-Jumbo Jockey Again a Heavy Hitter," *New York Post*, 1999.
77. Jay Searcy, Long-shot Charismatic Pulls Derby Surprise. Article. Philadelphia Inquirer, 1999
78. Neil Schmidt, "Derby Winner, Jockey Beat Long Odds," *The Cincinnati Enquirer*, May 2, 1999.
79. Elizabeth Mitchell, *Three Strides Before the Wire* (New York: Hyperion, 2002), 201.
80. Ibid.

Chapter 97

81. ABC Kentucky Derby Coverage, 1999 (Part 1): www.youtube.com/watch?v=Zim1Qr45_4c
82. Neil Schmidt, "Derby Winner, Jockey Beat Long Odds." *The Cincinnati Enquirer*, May 2, 1999.

Chapter 99

83. Jay Searcy, "Long-Shot Charismatic Pulls Derby Surprise," *Philly.com*, 1999.
84. The Associated Press, "Long-Shot Charismatic Races to Derby Victory," May 2, 1999.

Chapter 101

85. Bill Finley, "Lukas Gets Charismatic: Wayne Knows No. 4 Was Long Shot," *New York Daily News*, May 2, 1999.
86. Ibid.
87. Neil Schmidt, "Derby Winner, Jockey Beat Long Odds." *The Cincinnati Enquirer*, May 2, 1999.
88. Ibid.
89. Ed Fountaine, "Antley's Long, Hard Ride Jockey Overcomes Demons to Win Derby," New York Post, 1999
90. Ibid.
91. Jay Searcy, "Long-Shot Charismatic Pulls Derby Surprise," *Philly.com*, 1999.

Chapter 103

92. 1999 Kentucky Derby coverage. (Part 7): www.youtube.com/watch?v=KqMbddRoHEo
93. Chuck Culpepper, "Believe It: Antley Wins Again," *Lexington Herald-Leader*, November 28, 2001.
94. Ed Fountaine, "Antley's Long, Hard Ride Jockey Overcomes Demons to Win Derby," *New York Post*, 1999.

Chapter 105

95. Elizabeth Mitchell, *Three Strides before the Wire*, (New York: Hyperion, 2002), 91.

Chapter 106

96. YouTube. ABC coverage of Preakness (Part 6) www.youtube.com/watch?v=tYVs9AsaG1c
97. Ibid.

Chapter 107

98. Ed Fountaine and William Neuman, "Troubled Jockey Found Murdered," *New York Post*, December 4, 2000.

Chapter 108

99. ABC Coverage Preakness Stakes 1999 (Part 6): www.youtube.com/watch?v=tYVs9AsaG1c
100. Ibid.
101. Ibid.
102. ABC Coverage Preakness Stakes 1999 (Part 7) www.youtube.com/watch?v=lx6Q9M40ifY
103. Ibid.
104. "Charismatic Captures Preakness, Eyes Triple Crown," *Sports Illustrated*, June 3, 1999.
105. ABC Coverage Preakness Stakes 1999 (Part 7) www.youtube.com/watch?v=lx6Q9M40ifYIbid.
106. Ibid.

Chapter 109

107. Samantha Green, "History and Meaning of Carnations," www.proflowers.com/flowerguide/flowermeanings/carnation-meanings.aspx,3/17/2012

Chapter 110

108. Joe Drape, "For Charismatic's Camp: An Afternoon of Pain and Shock," *New York Times*, June 6, 1999,
109. ABC Coverage 1999 Belmont Stakes. (Part 1) www.youtube.com/watch?v=L31DgVxsh94
110. ABC Coverage 1999 Belmont Stakes. (Part 2) www.youtube.com/watch?v=fv9LnCo20B4
111. ABC Coverage 1999 Belmont Stakes. (Part 5) www.youtube.com/watch?v=8dL9Jxy1vUQ
112. Ibid.

Chapter 111

113. ABC Coverage 1999 Belmont Stakes (Part 6): www.youtube.com/watch?v=RtpePd1lzh8
114. Ibid.
115. Ibid.
116. Ed Fountaine, "Antley Defends His Antsy Belmont Ride," *New York Post*, June, 1999.
117. Ibid.
118. ABC Coverage 1999 Belmont Stakes (Part 6): www.youtube.com/watch?v=RtpePd1lzh8

Chapter 112

119. ABC Coverage Belmont Stakes (Part 2): www.youtube.com/watch?v=fv9LnCO20B4

Chapter 115

120. Richard Winton and Bill Christine, "Slain Jockey Recalled as Determined," *Los Angeles Times*, December 6, 2000.
121. Conversation with Michelle Antley, June, 2001.
122. David S. Jackson, "Death and the Horseman," *Time Magazine*, December 18, 2000.
123. Conversation with Michelle Antley, June, 2001.
124. Ed Fountaine, "Antley's Long, Hard Ride: Jockey Overcomes Demons to Win Derby," *New York Post*, 1999.

www.ingramcontent.com/pod-product-compliance
Lightning Source LLC
LaVergne TN
LVHW100300210926
848480LV00003B/973
* 9 7 9 8 2 1 8 6 8 6 1 9 2 *